"The sound of a shot and the splash of a duck had had the same effect on the Labrador as a trumpet call to an old war horse, and drew him as irresistibly. Without a second's hesitation he had plunged in for the retrieve, only to find he was unable to open his mouth to grasp the heavy duck properly, and was forced to tow it ashore by wingtip. He emerged from the water twenty feet from the man, the beautiful greenhead trailing from its outstretched wing, the sun striking the iridescent plumage. The Labrador looked doubtfully at the stranger, and Mackenzie stared back in open-mouthed amazement. For a moment the two were frozen in a silent tableau. . . ."
—Sheila Burnford, *The Incredible Journey*, 1971

Labs Afield

The Ultimate Tribute to the World's Greatest Retriever

Todd R. Berger, Editor
Photography by Alan and Sandy Carey

With stories by Jim Fergus, Gary Paulsen,
Bill Tarrant, Mel Ellis, Ron Schara,
John Barsness, E. Donnall Thomas, Jr.,
John Madson, John R. Wright,
and Paul A. Curtis

Voyageur Press

PetLife
LIBRARY

Compiled and edited by Todd R. Berger
Designed by Kjerstin Moody
Printed in Hong Kong

00   01   02   03   04   5   4   3   2   1

Library of Congress Cataloging-in-Publication Data available

ISBN 0-89658-489-5

Distributed in Canada by Raincoast Books, 9050 Shaughnessy Street, Vancouver, B.C. V6P 6E5

Published by Voyageur Press, Inc.
123 North Second Street
P.O. Box 338
Stillwater, MN 55082 U.S.A.
651-430-2210, fax 651-430-2211
books@voyageurpress.com
www.voyageurpress.com

Educators, fundraisers, premium and gift buyers, publicists, and marketing managers: Looking for creative products and new sales ideas? Voyageur Press books are available at special discounts when purchased in quantities, and special editions can be created to your specifications. For details contact the marketing department at 800-888-9653.

Permissions
We have made every effort to determine original sources and locate copyright holders of the excerpts in this book. Grateful acknowledgment is made to the writers, publishers, and agencies listed below for permission to reprint material copyrighted or controlled by them. Please bring to our attention any errors of fact, omission, or copyright.
"Ike: A Good Friend" from *My Life in Dog Years* by Gary Paulsen. Copyright © 1998 by Gary Paulsen. Reprinted by permission of Flannery Literary.
"Another Bend in the River" from *Pick of the Litter* by Bill Tarrant. Copyright © 1995 by Bill Tarrant. Reprinted by permission of The Lyons Press.
"A Close Call with the Dog Cops" by Jim Fergus. Copyright © 2000 by Jim Fergus. Reprinted by permission of the author.
"Guffy's Story" by John Madson. Copyright © 1994 by John Madson. Reprinted by permission of Dycie Madson.
"Passages" by E. Donnall Thomas, Jr. Copyright © 2000 by E. Donnall Thomas, Jr. Reprinted by permission of the author.
"The Dog that Hunts Anything" by John Barsness. Copyright © 1992 by John Barsness. Reprinted by permission of the author.
"Ducks and the Wings of Death" by Mel Ellis. Copyright © 1957 by *Field & Stream*. Reprinted by permission of the Sternig & Byrne Literary Agency.
"Gray Muzzles" by John R. Wright. Copyright © 1994 by John R. Wright. Reprinted by permission of the author.
"A Man and his Dog" by Ron Schara. Copyright © 1993 by Ron Schara. Reprinted by permission of the author.

PAGE 1: *A black Lab in a winter marsh in the American South.*

PAGE 2–3: *Calling for ducks at sunrise.*

PAGE 3, INSET: *A chocolate and a black Lab look skyward.*

FACING PAGE: *Most Labs are headed afield in autumn, but this yellow pup decided fall is an excellent time for a snooze among the decoys.*

PAGE 6: *Ever alert, a spectacular yellow Lab stands in an icy stream, ready to retrieve.*

ACKNOWLEDGMENTS

We would like to thank all of those who helped us with the photography for this book. In particular, we would like to thank Mark and Lisa Steingruber and their sons Brock and Nathan, Pete and Tanya Rothing at Diamond R Kennels, John and Laura McCarthy at Yellow Sporting Labs, Bill and Jamie Wood, Rod King, Joe Braverman, Curt Setzer, Jamie Benedict, John Haney and his son Jordan, Joel and Lori Davis, Russ James, Alan and Peggy Duda, Steve McDonnel, Bobby Joe Parker, Hal Booser, and Woody Bohannan.

A special thanks to Joe Skaggs and his Labs Courage and Susie. We had some great times together in the field watching and photographing his well-trained dogs work.

Many thanks also to Cal Horner, our neighbor up the street who has some wonderful black Labs, including our favorite, Lukey. Several times on short notice, Cal loaded up his dogs and headed for the field to catch that perfect photographic light.

A final thanks to Todd and Gwen Brittain and their daughter Gray Ann, owners of the Black Dog Hunting Club in Stuttgart, Arkansas, as well as Black Dog guides Jake Fisher, Trey Bohannan, and Mark Schupp. They were excellent hosts for over a week and helped us get some great photographs for this book. We strongly recommend them for a unique waterfowl hunting experience, complete with friendly hospitality and wonderful home-cooked meals (especially their thick, juicy steaks covered with mushrooms).

—ALAN AND SANDY CAREY

CONTENTS

INTRODUCTION

At the heart of wildfowling, a hunting Lab sits patiently waiting for you to shoot some birds. She is capable of doing things you can only dream of doing yourself: retrieving a pintail from an icy stream, finding and flushing a pheasant, or competing in a field trial. For the sportsman or -woman infatuated with gray skies full of soaring flocks of mallards, addicted to the whir of ruffed grouse flushed from an autumn covey, passionate about the field-trial circuit, the Labrador retriever is indispensable.

Surprisingly—perhaps shockingly—the Labrador retrievers as we know them today have only been around for a hundred and fifty years or so. With ancestry in Canada and development of the breed in Great Britain, large numbers of Labs did not arrive in the United States until the 1930s. Today they are not only the most popular hunting dog in the United States, but they are also the most popular dog of any kind, as measured by registrations with the American Kennel Club. Labs are also the most popular breed registered with the Canadian Kennel Club and the Kennel Club of the United Kingdom, and they rank very high in many other countries, as well. Some said it would be communism, others said it would be rock and roll, but as the new millennium begins, it is quite clear that the Labrador retriever has taken over the world.

And what are all these Labs doing? Giving horsey rides to tikes, doing their business all over your otherwise well-manicured backyard, chewing the legs off your chaise lounge? Well, yes. After all, the Lab is all dog. But while so many dog breeds, from the American cocker spaniel to the standard poodle, have had the passion for the hunt bred right out of their systems in efforts to meet the demand for these breeds as family pets, the Labrador retriever retains its lovable "friend-to-all" personality and still remains true to its soul—a world-class gun dog born to retrieve. As Richard A. Wolters notes in his classic book *Water Dog* (1964): "If you want a happy retriever, make him a worker; that's what he was bred for."

Indeed, the Labrador retriever *belongs* afield. Take him there.

After a successful retrieve, a black Lab with a soft mouth waits patiently for the hunter.

About *Labs Afield*

Labs Afield is a unique tribute to the hunting Labrador retriever. Other anthologies, including *Love of Labs* (1997), have taken a look at this wonderful breed as a lovable pet and as a cream-of-the-crop retriever, but no other book is squarely focused on the Lab as a hunting dog.

If you've spent a little time over the years reading the pages of *Field & Stream, Outdoor Life, Sports Afield, Ducks Unlimited,* and *Sports Illustrated,* you will recognize many of the venerable authors in this collection. *Labs Afield* includes a story by the late *Field & Stream* gun dog editor Bill Tarrant, a man who left a legacy of humane gun dog training that was not at all the norm when he first picked up a pen to defend the canine clans. There are also tales by Gary Paulsen, a celebrated author of dozens of novels, and Jim Fergus, author of two books that focus on his famed yellow Lab Sweetzer.

ABOVE: *A goofy pup mugs for the camera.*
FACING PAGE: *Teenage twin hunters call for ducks with their chocolate Lab.*
OVERLEAF: *A bumper-carrying pair of black Labs practice retrieving on a sunny autumn day.*

Also here is the work of many of the greatest scribes to write about Labs, including John Madson, E. Donnall Thomas, Jr., John Barsness, Paul A. Curtis, Mel Ellis, John R. Wright, and Ron Schara. These are writers who know the spirit of the hunting Lab best and have remarkable talent for capturing that spirit on paper.

Capturing the spirit of the Lab on film is the realm of Alan and Sandy Carey, Montana-based dog and nature photographers whose work has been widely published in magazines, calendars, and books. Tromping into an early winter marsh and standing thigh-deep in icy muck to capture just the right image of a frosty Lab returning with a pintail is what they do, and they do it exceptionally well.

You have your own memories of hunting with Labs. What better way to remember those great days in the field than to share *Labs Afield* with your Lab best friend? Put your feet up and call the dog to your side. It's time to begin.

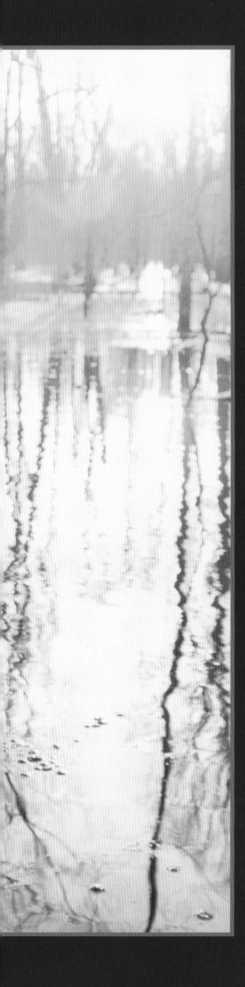

Part I

LABRADOR DAYS

"When my wife and I first moved to the Sonoran Desert, she used to say, 'It makes me feel like gold.' That's the way a Lab makes me feel. Their essence radiates through their pores."
—Bill Tarrant

LEFT: *Hunter and Lab watch the sun rise over flooded timber.*
ABOVE: *Bandannaed and jolly, a yellow Lab pauses in an autumn field.*

IKE:
A GOOD FRIEND

by Gary Paulsen

Days afield are a feast for the senses: Crisp autumn air, the sweet yet pungent smell of a reedy lakeshore, dawn breaking in the October sky. The setting would be incomplete without the beauty of a spectacular retrieve, the lick of a warm, slathery tongue, and the feel of wet fur as you stroke your Lab behind the ears. Not to mention the smell of a mucky dog snuggled up against you in a tiny blind. These are Labrador days.

Gary Paulsen knows days like this. At various times, the celebrated author has worked as a trapper, singer, and migrant farm worker, but he eventually found his niche as an author, having penned, remarkably, more than eighty books. Several of his books, including many tales of dogs and the hunt, were written for a juvenile audience.

"Ike: A Good Friend" first appeared in Paulsen's wonderful book *My Life in Dog Years* (1998).

A moment of reflection beside a placid stream.

MUCH OF MY childhood I was alone. Family troubles—my parents were drunks—combined with a devastating shyness and a complete lack of social skills to ensure a life of solitude. This isolation was not natural, of course, especially for a child, and most of the time I was excruciatingly lonely. I sought friends whenever I could, but was rarely successful.

When I was very young these times of aloneness were spent making model airplanes, reading comic books or just daydreaming. But when I was twelve, living in a small town named Twin Forks in northern Minnesota, an uncle gave me a Remington .22 rifle he'd bought at a hardware store for ten dollars. I ran to the woods.

It is not somehow "politically correct" to hunt, and that is a shame for young boys. For me it was not only the opening into a world of wonder, it was salvation. I lived and breathed to hunt, to fish.

Two rivers ran out of town, one to the north and one to the east, and any day, hour or few minutes I could spare I would run these rivers. The first year I hunted mostly rabbits and ruffed grouse—feeding myself in the process. I scuffled along in old boots with a box of .22 long rifle cartridges in my pocket and the single-shot rifle in my hand. On my back was an old army surplus light pack I'd bought with money from setting pins at the local bowling alley. In the pack I had matches, usually a loaf of bread, salt and an old aluminum pot for boiling water.

There was great beauty in running the rivers, especially in the fall when the leaves were turning. The maples were red gold and filtered the sunlight so that you could almost taste the richness of the light, and before long I added a surplus army blanket, rolled up over the pack, and I would spend the nights out as well. During school—where I did badly—I would hunt in the evenings. But on Friday I was gone, and I would frequently spend the entire weekend alone in the woods.

The problem was that I was alone. I had not learned then to love solitude—as I do now—and the feeling of loneliness was visceral, palpable. I would see something beautiful—the sun through the leaves, a deer moving through the dappled light, the explosion of a grouse flying up through the leaves—and I would turn to point it out to somebody, turn to say, "Look . . ." and there would be no one there.

The second fall after I'd started living in and off the woods I decided to hunt ducks. Miles to the north were the great swamps and breeding grounds of literally millions of ducks and geese, and when the migratory flights started south the sky would seem to darken with them. The .22 rifle was not suited for ducks—was indeed illegal for them—so I saved my money setting pins and bought an old single-shot Browning twelve-gauge shotgun from a kid named Sonny. The gun had a long barrel and a full choke, and with number four shot seemed to reach out forever. I never became really good with it, but could hit now and then when the ducks were flying at the right angle. Duck hunting soon became my life.

I did not have decoys but I made some blinds six miles out of town where there were cattail swamps. I would walk out there in the dark,

Full-bore ahead, a pheasant-toting Lab rises up and over a downed tree.

leaving the house at three in the morning, nestle into the blinds and wait for the morning flights to come in from the north. Usually I would get one or two ducks—once a goose—but some I wounded or didn't kill cleanly and they would get into the swamp grass and weeds in the water and I couldn't find them.

It was about then that I met Ike.

Ike was a great barrel-chested black Labrador that became one of the best friends I've ever had and was in all ways an equal; not a pet, not something to master, but an equal.

I had had other dogs. Snowball in the Philippines, then a cocker spaniel somebody gave me named Trina. They were sweet and dear and gave love the way only dogs can, with total acceptance, but Ike was the first dog I'd ever known not as a pet but as a separate entity, a partner.

We met strangely enough. It was duck season and I was going hunting. I woke up at three and sneaked from the basement, where I stayed when my parents were drunk—which was all the time—up into the kitchen. Quietly I made two fried egg sandwiches at the stove. I wrapped them in cellophane (this was well before sandwich bags), folded them into a paper sack and put them in my pack along with a Thermos of hot coffee. Then I got my shotgun from the basement. I dumped a box of shells into the pockets of the old

canvas coat I'd found in a trunk in the back of the coal room. I put on the knee-high rubber boots I'd bought at army surplus.

I walked from the apartment building four blocks to the railroad,

During a long, cold day in the field, a Lab is welcome for her companionship as much as her retrieving ability.

crossed the tracks near the roundhouse yard, crossed the Eighth Street bridge and then dropped down to the riverbank and started walking along the water.

The river quickly left settled country and headed into woods, and in the dark—there was just the faintest touch of gray on the horizon—it was hard going. The brush pulled at my clothes and after a mile and a half the swamps became more prevalent so that I was wading in muck. I

The imploring eyes and roly-poly bodies of these pups is endearing to even the coldest of hearts. And any hunter who has bonded with a Lab in the field will be endeared to the promise of retriever greatness that surely lies in their future.

went to pull myself up the bank and walk where the ground was harder.

It had been raining, mixed with snow, and the mud on the bank was as slick as grease. I fell once in the darkness, got to my feet and scrabbled up the bank again, shotgun in one hand and grabbing at roots and shrubs with the other. I had just gained the top, brought my head up over the edge, when a part of the darkness detached itself, leaned close to my face and went:

"Woof."

It was that distinct—not "arf," nor "ruff," nor a growl, but the very defined sound of "woof."

I was so startled that I froze, mouth half open. Then I let go of the shrub and fell back down the mud incline. On the way down the thought hit me—bear. Something big and black, that sound—it had to be a bear. Then the word *gun*. I had a gun. I landed on my back and aimed up the bank, pulled the hammer back and put my finger on the trigger before I realized the gun wasn't loaded yet. I never loaded it while walking in the dark. I clawed at my pockets for shells, found one, broke open the gun and inserted a shell, slammed it shut and was going to aim again when something about the shape stopped me. (It was well it did—I had accidentally jammed the barrel of the shotgun full of mud when I fell. Had I pulled the trigger the shell would have blown up in my face.)

There was just enough of the dawn to show a silhouette. Whatever it was remained at the top of the bank. It was sitting there looking down at me and was the wrong shape and size for a bear. It was a big dog, a black dog. But it was a dog and it wasn't attacking.

I lowered the gun and wiped the mud out of my eyes, stood and scraped mud off my clothes. I was furious, but not at the dog. There were other hunters who worked the river during duck season and some of them had dogs. I assumed that one of them was nearby and had let his animal run loose, scaring about ten years off my life.

"Who owns you?" I asked the shape. It didn't move or make any

Water whipping from his tail, a yellow Lab comes ashore with his retrieve.

Why have just one Lab when you can have seventeen?

further sounds and I climbed the bank again and it moved back a few feet, then sat again.

"Hello!" I called into the woods around me. "I have your dog here!"

There was nobody.

"So you're a stray?" There were many stray dogs in town and some of them ran to the woods. It was bad when they did because they often formed packs and did terrible damage. In packs they were worse than wolves because they did not fear men the way wolves did and they tore livestock and some people to pieces.

But strays were shy and usually starved. This dog stayed near me and in the gathering light I could see that he was a Labrador and that he was well fed. His coat was thick and he had fat on his back and sides.

"Well," I said. "What do I do with you?"

This time his tail thumped twice and he pointedly looked at the gun, then back at my face, then down the side of the river to the water.

"You want to hunt?"

There, he knew that word. His tail hammered his sides and he stood, wiggling, and moved off along the river ahead of me.

I had never hunted with a dog before and did not know for certain what was expected of me. But I started to follow, thinking we might jump up a mallard or teal. Then I remembered my fall and the mud and that the gun was still loaded. I unloaded it and checked the bore and found the end packed with mud. It took me a minute to clean it out and reload it and before I'd finished he'd come back and sat four feet away, watching me quietly.

A blocky-headed chocolate Lab in an early winter field.

It was light enough now for me to see that he had a collar and a tag so he wasn't a stray. It must be some town dog, I thought, that had followed me. I held out my hand. "Come here . . ."

But he remained at a distance and when it was obvious that I was ready to go he set off again. It was light enough now to shoot—light enough to see the front bead of the shotgun and a duck against the sky—so I kept the gun ready and we had not gone fifty yards when two mallards exploded out of some thick grass near the bank about twenty yards away and started up and across the river.

It was a classic shot. Mallards flying straight up to gain altitude before making off, backlit against a cold, cloudy October sky. I raised the gun, cocked it, aimed just above the right-hand duck to lead his flight and squeezed the trigger.

There was a crash and the recoil slammed me back. I was small and the gun was big and I usually had a bruise after firing it more than once. But my aim was good and the right-hand duck seemed to break in the air, crumpled and fell into the water. I had shot ducks over the river before and the way to get them was to wait until the current brought the body to shore. Sometimes it took most of the morning, waiting for the slow-moving water to bring them in.

This time was different. With the smell of powder still in the air, almost before the duck finished failing, the dog was off the bank in a great leap, hit the water swimming, his shoulders pumping as he churned the surface and made a straight line to the dead duck. He took it in his mouth gently, turned and swam back, climbed the bank and put the duck by my right foot, then moved off a couple of feet and sat, looking at me.

I made sure the duck was dead, then picked it up and tied it to my belt with a string I carried for the purpose. The dog sat and watched me the whole time, waiting. It was fully light now and I moved to him, petted him—he let me but in a reserved way—and pulled his tag to the side so I could read it.

My name is Ike.

That's all it said. No address, no owner's name, just one short sentence.

"Well, Ike"—at this his tail wagged—"I'd like to thank you for bringing me the duck . . ."

And that was how it started, how I came to know Ike.

Duck season soon consumed me and I spent every morning walking and hunting the river. On school days I would go out and come back just in time to get to classes and on the week- ends I stayed out.

And every morning Ike was there. I'd come across the bridge, start down the river, and he'd be there, waiting. After a few mornings he'd let me pet him—I think he did it for me more than him—and by the end of the first week I was looking forward to seeing him. By the middle of the second week I felt as if we'd been hunting with each other forever.

A Lab with this kind of power in his hindquarters is likely to jump right over the pond.

And he knew hunting. Clearly somebody had trained him well. He moved quietly, sat in the blind with me without moving, watched the barrel of the gun to see which duck I was going to shoot at, and when I shot he would leap into the water. On those occasions when I missed—I think more often than not—he would watch the duck fly away, turn to me and give me a look of such uncompromising pity and scorn that I would feel compelled to apologize and make excuses.

"The wind moved the barrel," or "A drop of water hit my eye when I shot."

Of course, he did not believe me but would turn back, sitting there waiting for the next shot so I could absolve myself.

When the hunting was done he'd walk back with me to town, trotting alongside, until we arrived at the bridge. There he would stop and sit down and nothing I did would make him come farther. I tried waiting him out to see where he would go but when it was obvious that I wasn't going to leave he merely lay down and went to sleep, or turned and started back into the woods, looking back to see if we were

A boy and his dog goof around among the decoys.

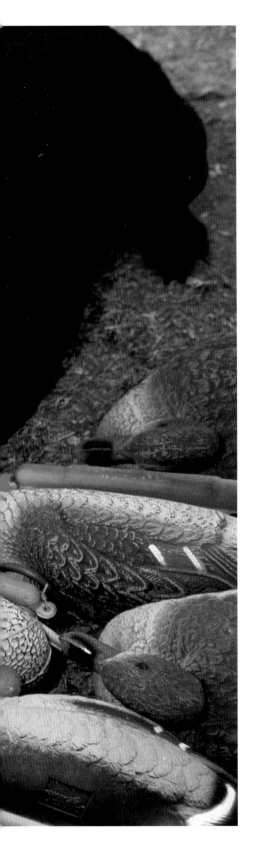

going hunting again.

Once I left him, crossed the bridge and then hid in back of a building and watched. He stayed until I was out of sight and then turned and trotted north away from the bridge along the river. There were no houses in that direction, at least on the far side of the river, and I watched him until he disappeared into the woods. I was no wiser than I had been.

The rest of his life was a mystery and would remain so for thirty years. But when we were together we became fast friends, at least on my part.

I would cook an extra egg sandwich for Ike and when the flights weren't coming we would "talk." That is to say, I would talk, tell him all my troubles, and he would sit, his enormous head sometimes resting on my knee, his huge brown eyes looking up at me while I petted him and rattled on.

On the weekends when I stayed out, I would construct a lean-to and make a fire, and he would curl up on the edge of my blanket. Many mornings I would awaken to find him under the frost-covered blanket with me, sound asleep, my arm thrown over him, his breath rumbling against my side.

It seemed like there'd always been an Ike in my life and then one morning he wasn't there and I never saw him again. I tried to find him. I would wait for him in the mornings by the bridge, but he never showed again. I thought he might have gotten hit by a car, or his owners moved away. I mourned him and missed him. But I did not learn what happened to him for thirty years.

I grew and went into the crazy parts of life, army and those other mistakes a young man could make. I grew older and got back into dogs, this time sled dogs, and ran the Iditarod race across Alaska. After my first run I came back to Minnesota with slides of the race to show to all the people who had supported me. A sporting goods store had been one of my sponsors and I gave a public slide show of the race one evening.

There was an older man sitting in a wheelchair and I saw that when I told a story of how Cookie, my lead dog, had saved my life his eyes teared up and he nodded quietly.

When the event was over he wheeled up to me and shook my hands.

"I had a dog like your Cookie—a dog that saved my life."

"Oh—did you run sleds?"

He shook his head. "No. Not like that. I lived up in Twin Forks when I was young and was drafted to serve in the Korean War. I had a Labrador that I raised and hunted with, and left him when I went away. I was gone just under a year; I got wounded and lost the use of my legs. When I came back from the hospital he was waiting there and he spent the rest of his life by my side. I would have gone crazy without him. I'd sit for hours and talk to him and he would listen quietly . . . it was so sad. He loved to hunt and I never hunted again." He faded off and his eyes were moist again. "I still miss him . . ."

I looked at him, then out the window of the sporting goods store. It was spring and the snow was melting outside but I was seeing fall and a boy and a Lab sitting in a duck blind. Twin Forks, he'd said—and the Korean War. The time was right, and the place, and the dog.

"Your dog," I said. "Was he named Ike?"

He smiled and nodded. "Why, yes—but how . . . did you know him?"

There was a soft spring rain starting and the window misted with it. That was why Ike had not come back. He had another job.

"Yes," I said, turning to him. "He was my friend. . . ."

FACING PAGE: *Power emanates from a chocolate Lab on a frosty Montana morning.*

OVERLEAF: *Autumn sunshine warms the sleek, healthy coat of a beautiful black Lab.*

ANOTHER BEND IN THE RIVER

by Bill Tarrant

The late Bill Tarrant dedicated his life to dogs in general and Labrador retrievers in particular. The author of thirteen books on dogs, including *Hey Pup, Fetch It Up!* (1979), *The Magic of Dogs* (1995), and *Retriever Pups: The Formative First Year* (1999), Tarrant served as the gun dog editor for *Field & Stream* magazine for more than twenty-five years. He is widely recognized as the pioneer in humane gun dog training; he believed that "domination in gun dog training is dead" and that if a trainer bonds with his dog, "a look of disappointment on the trainer's face hurts an errant dog more than if he had been beat down by a 2 x 4."

Jarringly blunt at times, Tarrant also wrote elegantly of days afield. "Another Bend in the River" is such a tale. Originally appearing in *Field & Stream,* the story was later included in Tarrant's book *Pick of the Litter* (1995).

A morning hunt for ducks along a western river.

THE PRAIRIE MIND is inflexibly simple and correct. It cannot acknowledge the Arkansas River being pronounced any other way. Up at the river's headwaters, high in the Rockies, people may mistakenly call it the Arkansa(w). And down in the state of Arkansa(w), where the river empties into the Mississippi, those people may lose their (s) and say it the same way. But when that river enters Kansa(s), we hold to that (s) ending with the grip of a badger. If we didn't, then our state would be Kansa(w), and that would be unimaginable.

The farm ponds in Kansas are frozen now, and the waterfowl on the open refuges seldom leave their government handouts to forage the storm-shattered and snow-ladened fields. So the fifteen-month-old black Lab pup I call Happy walks the banks of the Arkansas River with me, up by Great Bend, Kansas. For the river makes a great bend here, and like ant trails that bend this way or that, you can never reason its going. And though the river is frozen in sections, still there are open spots where a chance duck may idle and feed.

Happy rambles with that rolling of baby fat about his shoulders, the snow and ice on his coat glistening in the bright but heatless sun. Happy doesn't know why we're out here—why we're not hidden in the hay bales by the farm pond or sneaking corners of this shallow river in the old johnboat with the bottom slicked by the scum of stinkbait and the rusted metal fish stringer still snapped to the oar lock.

At those spots where the bank is nearly level with the river, Happy runs down to wade in the water midst floating ice to drink. Where the bank is high and undercut, he stands and looks quizzically at the brown swirls, his mind still vacant about what he sees.

The earth is frozen, and where the wind's blown it clean of snow I walk without drag, the Christmas parka in winter-camo pattern prompting me to see myself as a snow leopard. Thought of the big cat brings an imagined spring to my step, puts me up on my toes.

The heft of the Remington automatic swings easily in my right hand. It'll mount in a second, swing as fast. It'll bark and bite and a redlegged mallard (the red legs are always last to come down from Canada) will lie flat on his back in the water, and Happy will have to hope that's where the bank meets the river. Happy's unsure about leaping from a high bank.

But the pup's signed on as a gun dog, and he'll have to meet life as the hunter finds it: The hours of nothing, the seconds of plenty—the clear shot, the shot deflected through gnarled cottonwood limbs, the birds flying close to the cut bank, not to clear for fifty yards before they lift. And who's got a gun that can shoot fifty yards? Oh, I may have done it once or twice.

I labor under a four-strand barbed wire fence (no longer a lithe snow leopard), to leave behind the frozen winter wheatfield. There'll be cattle here, but Happy won't tend to them. He's learned that since puppyhood while we were out in the fields Happy Timing. There's nothing harder to walk in than a pasture where cattle have sunk in during heavy rains; the frozen escarpments always catch a toe of your

A Lab waits patiently for his call to action alongside a half-frozen pond.

boot and plunge you forward. And the wire fence now runs along the river bank, so Happy will have to duck under to make any retrieve. But he's learned that Happy Timing, too.

Matter of fact, Happy knows it all: all the cover and terrain and hazards and distractions. That's what we learned all summer walking in the idle fields. All Happy doesn't know is the red-legged mallard floating upside down in the water.

I kneel and call the pup to side, telling him in serious voice to stay low, not to kick out sideways, not to go on a lark. For the bend in the river lies just ahead—there'll be a stretch of open water there. The ducks will feed against the bank out of the wind, and any sentinel they post will be able to see everywhere except over the cut bank. So dog and man must always slink around bends in rivers. They must disappear. Yet, all humped over, how can a man move fast? For when the ducks do sense your presence they'll scat, since they've got this all figured out. They know the gun. They've met guns all the way from Canada to Kansas. They are experts on guns. They know how long it takes to shoulder them, how far they shoot, how wide their pattern.

All I've done is walk hunched over and I'm winded. Still, Happy and I move quickly forward, his puppy mind sensing this is different, this is serious. His puppy eyes are no longer vacant; they are intense about he does not know what. And suddenly they're on us: that's right, not us on them but them on us. A flight of seven mallards has cut across my left shoulder; they were making their way for the open water and must have been daydreaming, for they tried to set down right beside us. And now the gun won't raise nor sweep in a second, and when it's finally up it won't shoot. I forget the safety. And Happy's running after the ducks. The flying-away ducks.

And I can't believe it. But I must. Always it's this way. For that's hunting. To have everything planned, and then it's you who gets blown out of the water. It is myself I see float belly up in my snow leopard coat down the murky river.

But I can't think of that! Happy's turned from the flying ducks and now runs straight toward a herd of cattle. The ducks never saw me, I never saw the Herefords. I'm on the whistle, telling Happy to come back when right from below me, right from the cut bank I was to have stalked, spring up three mallards in grating voice and a fountain of water. They hang in the air before me like tethered balloons. They can't gain loft, their wings miss the wind, and I am paralyzed. The whole world laughs at me. The ducks, the cattle, and Happy all laugh, for that's how Happy got his name.

And now the cattle come charging in that straight-legged way they have. Only I'm not laughing. I don't take to unraveling all that well, to see precision dragged out by dry bearings, to see the whole engine of life explode. So I run straight at the cattle, giving a call the Kiowa must have yelled at buffalo. And it looks like we're going to collide when suddenly the cattle feel they're in the presence of a bona fide idiot and they swing off, churning the frozen ground to lift in fist-sized clods.

FACING PAGE: *Hunter and black Lab on the alert for ducks.*

Boom! A yellow Lab explodes into a stream in late fall.

Now Happy can chase them. And I blow the whistle.

I sit on the dried, chunked mud and wait for Happy to run out his string. Finally he comes, covered with the foam of his lust, his tongue hanging limp. I can't scold him. I introduced him to cattle when Happy Timing, but I never put him behind a stampede. He goes past me to the river and walks midst the ice floes to drink. But he looks back with too much white in his eyes. He is concerned about me. I may scold him. So I must shake it off for both of us. I toss a dried cow chip out behind him, and he leaps and pumps to make the retrieve.

But the cow chip goes with the water's current, and suddenly Happy goes faster than he can swim. He tries to turn toward the bank, but he enters swirls, and I can imagine all those forces as they press against him. Yet, he snatches the cow chip and leaps from the water to his waist, then twists and turns toward the bank, crabbing now to come in straight. I never taught him that. Survival put that in him. I take the slickened cow chip from his mouth and drop it to the ground, covering it with my boot, telling him, "No." But I must push his head back with my other boot. Finally he looks into my eyes for a long time, then turns and ambles to go shake water, a rainbow of light arching about his shoulders.

I should let him rest a minute, so I pat my pockets to find the candy bar. I chew on it as I look off to the horizon, off to the grain elevators that accent the flat prairie floor from Texas to Canada. They look like great silver trophies erected to

"Well done, friend." A hunter stoops to scratch his Lab on the scruff of the neck after a successful retrieve.

the farmer and his kin. But that was before man and nature devastated the farmer. Now the silos stand as tombstones.

There were two American statesmen who knew about these grain elevators, though they never saw one. Throughout their political lives they maintained a running debate both bitter and crucial.

Alexander Hamilton said the future of America was the city artisan, the shopkeeper, their urban interests would both foster and protect a strong national government. Thomas Jefferson pleaded, "No, the future of this land lies in the hands of the family farmer and home rule. That is the basis of democracy. Lose them and you lose it all."

I'm thinking about naming my next dog Jefferson when I give Happy the last bite of candy and cast out with an empty hand, telling him to "Hie on." He leaps high to tap my chest with his front paws and twists to come down going away from me. Running now.

Again the gun rests easy in my hand. Again my steps grow certain. But still, I glance back now and then. I've been am-bushed once. And I see the cattle move up slowly on a knoll to watch after us. They were ambushed, too.

Happy runs happy after he knows not what. And I pick up my pace knowing game cannot be far away. For there's always another bend in the river.

ABOVE: *A black, a chocolate, and a yellow Lab scan the skies for geese.* OVERLEAF: *Young but serious, a chocolate Lab pup is ready to get down to business.*

A Close Call
with the Dog Cops

by Jim Fergus

Jim Fergus is a longtime correspondent for *Outside* magazine and a contributing editor for *Sports Afield.* A prolific freelance writer, Fergus has published his work in numerous magazines and newspapers, including *Newsweek,* the *Paris Review, Esquire, Texas Monthly,* and the *Denver Post.* He has written two books featuring his now famous yellow Lab Sweetzer, *A Hunter's Road* (1992), one of the best-selling bird hunting books of all time, and *The Sporting Road* (1999). As Fergus says today, "I owe the past decade of my writing career to Sweetzer. Although I've always been an avid fisherman, I didn't even pick up a shotgun until I was 39 years old and suddenly found myself with a dog who demanded I take her hunting." His Sweetzer-led trips afield became fodder for much of his writing.

As Fergus knows through Sweetzer's insistence, a hunting Lab belongs in the field, but sometimes the circumstances of a Lab owner's life carry a Lab far from the marshes, wild ducks, and hidden coveys.

"A Close Call with the Dog Cops" is just such a tale of a dog out of water.

A black Lab, retrieving bumper in mouth, practices her technique on a sunny day.

I DON'T KNOW what got into me, but for one reason or another I decided recently that my wife and I needed some urban influence in our lives. I will be the first to admit that I am a hopeless country bumpkin—a rube, a hayseed, a hick, a yokel; I've hated cities all my life and have gone to some extraordinary lengths to avoid them.

But I think it was the Spanish poet Lorca who said something to the effect that the well-rounded man must at some point cover himself in the "red dust" of the city—air pollution I guess—and so I shook the cow manure off my boots and off we went to live in an apartment in town. Of course I go nowhere without my yellow Lab, Sweetzer, but we had been assured that dogs were welcome in this particular building.

Sweetz and I were homesick right off for the Big Open but we made the best of things, taking long walks every afternoon in the city park. Like many American cities these days, this one had a "goose problem"—hundreds, thousands of Canada geese had taken up residence in the city parks and on the golf courses. Ironically, one of the great success stories of modern wildlife management—the restoration of goose populations—has become a kind of urban nightmare. Now there were too many geese; the park and golf courses looked like a scene from Alfred Hitchcock's *The Birds*. There were geese everywhere, there was goose poop everywhere, and the birds themselves were a sorry, half-domesticated version of their former wild selves. They spent a lot of time loafing around the scummy city ponds and generally making a nuisance of themselves. They didn't even migrate south anymore. Every now and then they'd just fly over to the nearest golf course to eat some fertilized/herbicized golf course grass.

Of course, to a hunter the obvious solution would be to allow some kind of controlled goose hunting on the golf courses, maybe even on special days in the park (Hunters Day!), but it goes without saying that such a concept will never fly in urban America and so instead the recreation department of the city spends many thousands of dollars each year trying to trap the excess geese and transplant them to places where they can be legally hunted. However, having by then grown accustomed to easy city living, and the amenities it offers, most of these urban geese simply fly back to town at the first opportunity.

So Sweetz and I took long walks every afternoon in the city park. I often took her off the leash because she is quite capable of walking at heel without it, and sometimes I would throw a tennis ball for her to retrieve. Every now and then I even let her make a rush, a kind of playful feint, at the park geese. With no natural predators in the city, I thought it might help keep them on their toes, and she never actually nailed any.

One day early on, another man in the park walking his dog, a terrier, stopped me. I don't know how he knew we weren't from around there but he obviously did. I may as well have had a sign taped to my forehead: "*Country bumpkin. Kick me.*"

A Labrador retriever ready to hunt in the American Midwest.

"It's none of my business," the fellow said, "but you know the Dog Police will give you a ticket for letting your dog off the leash."

"The Dog Police?" I answered, "But she's not bothering anyone, she's right at heel."

"That doesn't matter," he said. "It's a seventy dollar fine if they catch you with your dog off the leash."

"What do these Dog Cops look like?" I asked.

"The drive around in recreation department vans," the man said, "and most of them are mean little bastards who love to write tickets." (It's true that it takes a certain temperament to be a Dog Cop.)

That same day in the park I saw a woman throwing a ball for her young Lab to retrieve. I approached her. "Aren't you afraid of getting busted by the Dog Cops?" I asked.

"Oh, I get busted all the time," she said. "I get at least one ticket a month. But this dog is six months old and he needs to run, and so I just consider it a basic pet expense—like going to the vet."

I hadn't actually seen the Dog Police yet but now I was getting paranoid. I still let Sweetz off the leash but I spent a lot of time looking over my shoulder. And I started hearing more and more Dog Cop horror stories from my city friends and acquaintances.

One evening after work, Dave Williams, for instance, who owns a brace of well-trained English springer spaniel hunting dogs, took them to his tiny neighborhood park. The park had a small pond; it was late in

ABOVE: *A trio of happy Labs ready for mischief.*
FACING PAGE: *Water churning above and behind him, a yellow Lab retrieves a stick tossed into a Montana lake.*

Lab puppies in three flavors lounging around in a pile of duck decoys.

the day—nearly dusk—and no one else was there. Dave looked around, thought the coast was clear, unhooked the dogs from their leashes, tossed a couple of retriever dummies into the water, and sent his dogs for them. All the while the Dog Police had been watching him through binoculars from their van, and by the time his dogs had retrieved the dummies to hand, Dave was being written up for not one, but two, tickets, seventy dollars apiece—one for each leashless dog.

And one day, the Dog Police came right to my friend Bob Stanley's door. Evidently someone in his neighborhood had complained about Bob's dogs barking and now a Dog Cop stood at his door demanding to see the vaccination and registration papers for his dogs.

"I hope you told him to go screw himself," I said, outraged, when Bob told me this story. "Did you ask him if he had a search warrant?"

"No, I didn't," Bob said with resignation. "Jim, the guy was packing."

"The Dog Cop had a gun?"

"Yeah, and of course, my registration papers weren't exactly in order," Bob said. "By the time it was over, it cost me almost three hundred bucks."

All in a day's work: Mucky and mottled, a yellow Lab slop-slops along a shoreline.

Now I was really getting paranoid. I started having nightmares about the Dog Gestapo knocking on my door in the middle of the night, demanding to see Sweetzer's city registration papers, which, it goes without saying, we do not have. And so they drag her away, howling, to languish in a sunless cell in Dog Prison.

And then one day it happened. Sweetz was off the leash in the park; we weren't bothering anyone, she was perfectly under control, she wasn't even chasing the geese, she was just retrieving a tennis ball that I had thrown in order to give her a little exercise, when the Dog Cops pulled up in their van, two of them descending from either side. The were small, stocky, swarthy fellows in uniforms that included shorts and black boots, and one had his ticket pad out and neither of them looked one bit friendly.

By now Sweetz was back at heel, but she didn't like the aggressive way in which the Dog Cops were approaching us, and she started growling at them.

"Bad idea!" I whispered to her. "Knock it off!"

"Your dog is off the leash," the Dog Cop said. "I'm going to have to write you up."

"Yeah, o.k.," I said. I didn't want any trouble.

"I need some identification," he said. "I don't see a tag on your dog's collar."

"She's a hunting dog," I said. "She doesn't wear tags, they tend to get hung up when she goes through fences."

"I need proof of city registration," he said.

"I haven't got it," I said. "We're not from around here." Which wasn't completely untrue.

"Then I have to see your driver's license, sir," said the Dog Cop.

"I don't have my driver's license. I didn't bring my wallet. We're just taking a walk in the park."

"In that case, I'm going to have to impound your dog," he said, "until you can provide some identification."

"Yeah, right," I said defiantly.

City Labs may have to content themselves with fetching a Flippy Flopper, though a hunting Lab will be satisfied with nothing less than feathers in her mouth.

"You and six other little guys just like you." It was my worst urban nightmare come true.

"Ramon, get the noose on that dog," the Dog Cop said to his partner. Clearly, he wasn't fooling around.

But before Ramon could do so, I hollered: "Run Sweetz!" And the two of us took off across the park, running for our lives.

Ramon pursued us on foot, while the head Dog Cop—I never did learn his name—jumped in the van. I heard a siren start up. I glanced over my shoulder to see Ramon speaking into a walky-talky as he ran. This cost him valuable time, while Sweetz and I, both of us in tiptop hunting condition, sprinted ahead.

We kept to the middle of the park where the van couldn't follow, and where there were lots of other people. Other park recreators turned to watch us impassively as we fled, as urbanites will do, and a few dog walkers shouted words of encouragement as we passed, because everyone hates the Dog Cops.

Sweetz and I have been in some tough spots before. We've faced giant swamp rats in Alabama, alligators in Florida; we've had close encounters with bears in Colorado, rattlers in Idaho; we've been lost in the wilds of Wisconsin and headwalled on a cliff in Utah. But this was the first time we'd ever been fugitives from the law.

The pleading eyes of a Lab who would rather be afield.

At last we managed to elude the Dog Cops, losing Ramon in an alley and making our way back home, where we triple locked the door of the apartment. For the next few days we only went out at night, and of course, we stayed away from the park. Even so, I wore dark glasses and a hat when we ventured forth, and Sweetz assumed her Shar-pei disguise. (Many Lab owners have discovered that if you take hold of your dog's head with both hands and kind of bunch the skin up and pull it forward, they are dead ringers for the wrinkled Chinese breed. A little surgical tape to hold things in place, and voilà!)

Finally we decided the city was no place for a hunter and a hunter's dog. Under cover of night, we loaded up the Airstream and headed back to the open country.

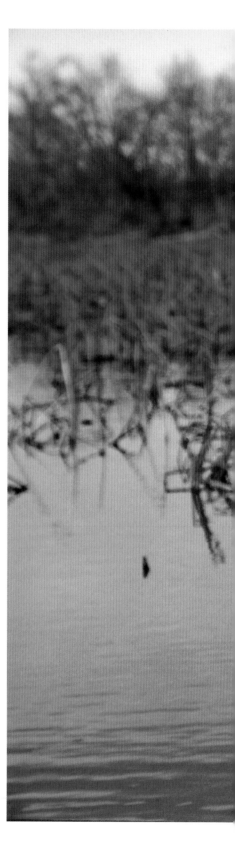

Back in his element, a black Labrador retriever stands at the ready in a blind.

Part II

THE HEART OF A CHAMPION

*"Almost everyone was soon calling
[the Lab] One, short for number one because
that's what he looked like right from the start."*
—Gene Hill, "One" from *Tears and Laughter,* 1981

LEFT: *A day's hunt in an icy marsh lies ahead for this eager
Lab.*
ABOVE: *Husband and wife and their pair of yellow Labs,
hunting in the American West.*

GUFFY'S STORY

by John Madson

Every Lab has a little of the champion in him, though that may be hard to believe when your Lab ignores a whistle command, runs for cover when a shot is fired, or nonchalantly eats the mallard you sent him to retrieve. Still, his heart is in the right place. And if given half a chance, most Labs will rise to the occasion, exhibiting championship qualities that will spawn countless tales of daring retrieves at the corner bar. The Labrador retriever is a champion by nature.

The late Illinois outdoors writer John Madson knew something about Labrador champions, as well as many other aspects of a life spent afield. During a quarter century working for the Winchester-Western Conservation Division of the Olin Corporation and later as a full-time freelance writer, Madson penned numerous tales of dogs, hunting, and game animals for magazines such as *Audubon, Smithsonian,* and *National Geographic.* He also published five books, including *Stories from Under the Sky* (1961), *Out Home* (1979), and *Up on the River* (1985).

"Guffy's Story" originally appeared in the November/December 1994 issue of *Ducks Unlimited.*

A burly chocolate Lab up to his haunches in a marsh.

THE ONLY TIME I ever saw Timothy John Lindboom's full name was when his application crossed my desk. To the world at large, he was simply "T.J." The same brevity extended to his dog, the black Labrador retriever that was registered as "McGuffy" but answered to "Guffy."

Good call names should be short—easily yelled, heard, and remembered. And in the bleak marsh-world of wildfowling where courage and loyalty are common virtues, the call names "T.J." and "Guffy" would stand for those virtues to an uncommon degree.

His application was for the hunting preserve management training course we were running at Nilo Farms. T.J. hoped to start a preserve of his own someday, and figured we could teach him a lot of what he'd need to know. He was also deeply interested in Labrador retrievers and wanted to work with some of the best.

On both counts, the five-month training program filled the bill. Nilo Farms was a demonstration and experimental hunting preserve in southwestern Illinois, owned by the Winchester-Western Division of the Olin Corporation and run by W-W's Conservation Department. Dr. Ed Kozicky was director of the tight little outfit; I was Ed's segundo. Our assignment was to promote professional game management in general, and quality hunting preserve management in particular. Hence the job training program on Nilo's 700 acres of timber, fields, and little lakes inhabited by game birds, gun dogs, and hunters using nothing but red shells. Some job. Not heaven, maybe, but close.

T.J. and his wife, Debby, came there from Oregon in 1976—a handsome couple in their mid-20s and looking years younger than they really were. Between them on the seat of the old pickup truck was two-year-old Guffy, who had been delivered to them as a small puppy on their first wedding anniversary. T.J. joined the Nilo crew on October 1 and Debby found a teaching job in the local school system.

They rented an old farmhouse not far from Nilo. It wasn't much, but was all they could afford. Some of their furniture ran to recycled orange crates. Still, the place was cheap, convenient, and had seven acres of hills and water that T.J. figured was "just about perfect for training a dog."

Guffy's retrieving skills were already awesome.

At less than a year old, he placed in the first licensed field trial he ever entered. A year later he ran in the National Amateur and soon became an Amateur Field Champion. In mid-September, a few weeks before T.J. reported at Nilo, Guffy won back-to-back open and amateur licensed trials in Wisconsin.

One of the prime reasons for T.J.'s interest in our training program was Nilo Kennels, the domain of nearly a hundred Labradors and bird dogs, with four full-time dog handlers headed by T.W. "Cotton" Pershall, the dean of professional retriever trainers. The nickname derived from his shock of blond hair. He was never called by his registered name "Theodore." Not twice, anyway.

Cotton and T.J. hit it off from the start.

Two Labs find a dry spot in the middle of an icy stream.

The old pro was a rich lode of retriever savvy—but mining it wasn't easy. Cotton never volunteered information and would simply ignore foolish questions. Not that he was antisocial or arrogant; he just didn't choose to waste time on idiots. But if you knew what to ask, Cotton would tell you what you wanted to know. T.J. not only asked the right questions in the right way, but had a young dog that deserved the best answers.

I can hear Cotton yet, on the subject of one-dog amateurs like T.J.:

"Hey, they can be rough!" he'd say in his soft Arkansas drawl, shaking his head in mock despair. "Man, they can kill you in an open trial. Ain't got but the one dog and they spend all their time with it. I mean, all their time! Look at me. Fifty-sixty dogs to work with. Even if I get 'em culled down to a few, ain't no way I can get as close to any one of 'em as a one-dog man can."

Still, he never let that interfere with helping T.J. with Guffy. Cotton soon saw that the dog was making an exceptional effort

Tongue lolling, a yellow Lab catches his breath during a hunt on the Great Plains.

to communicate with his owner, and helped T.J. bridge the gap. That's what I remember most about those two: man and dog heading out into the field side by side, talking together in their special way, each understanding the other.

That Guffy was something to see. He really was.

I remember little things. Like T.J. and Cotton working their dogs late one afternoon over at Buck Lake and Guffy being sent on a long blind retrieve. Too long, as it turned out. Guffy took a beautiful line but when T.J. tried to check him with the whistle, the dog didn't respond.

"He's never refused like that before," T.J. said. "What's wrong with him?"

"Nothing wrong with your dog," Cotton replied. "He just outran the whistle, is all. Can't hear you. Get a louder one!"

By the time he came to Nilo, Guffy had accumulated 100 All-Age points in tough competition and had begun to gain recognition as a contender for the National Championship Stake. The 1976 National was being held near Albuquerque, New Mexico, that November—and T.J. figured it might be time for the biggest test of all. Cotton talked to Doc Kozicky about it, and Doc agreed that it was a good idea. He gave T.J. his blessing, some time off, advanced some travel money—and

Guffy and T.J. headed for New Mexico.

The National Championship Stake usually consisted of 10 series of tests spread over five days of intense competition. Just being there as a qualified contender with some of the world's finest retrievers is a singular honor. Surviving through half of the 10 series is a star in any dog's crown—and Guffy completed seven series before he was eliminated. Cotton was there, and saw it.

"Guffy did just fine," he told me. "It was T.J.'s fault, and you can't really blame him, either. That's an awful lot of pressure on a young handler."

T.J.'s disappointment was especially bitter, knowing that he had let his dog down. "It was a real sharp angle on a water test, and I gave Guffy a bad angle. I just kind of fouled him up myself." Heartsick and disgusted with himself, he left before the trial was over. Other owners and handlers wanted him to stay, but he couldn't. How could he hang around, watching dogs that were no better than the fine retriever he'd betrayed with his poor handling?

So he headed back to Nilo instead, hoping to get there before Thanksgiving. He was making time on a divided highway in the Texas panhandle when disaster struck.

A young Lab, still eager to hunt, sits in the boat with decoys and ducks after a day of waterfowling.

"It was near Amarillo at dawn. I saw headlights coming, and then I saw this pickup truck sideswiping a car. There were sparks flying. The car shot straight over into the lane I was in. The people in the pickup were illegal aliens from Mexico, and drunk. They were all going very fast, because the people in the car were trying to outrun the drunks."

Out of control and into T.J.'s lane, the car hit him head-on. He was thrown through the windshield and then back into the seat again, with broken ribs and broken right femur. Guffy had been sitting in the seat beside him when the engine came through the fire wall and struck the dog. His injuries were remarkably similar to his master's, with broken ribs, broken right femur, and a smashed pelvis. The dog's broken leg was more serious than T.J.'s, however, for the femur's head was crushed.

When everything had stopped moving, T.J. grabbed the dog by the choke chain and Guffy pulled his master out of the wrecked car and onto the ground where they lay together in shock.

T.J. clung to consciousness, and to his dog. "I had to hold onto Guffy; I knew he was badly hurt and didn't want him running off to be run over by a car.

ABOVE: *Tip-toeing across a stream, a black Lab returns with a retrieving dummy.*
FACING PAGE: *A cannonball water entry for a yellow Lab intent on the retrieve.*
OVERLEAF: *A perch above the water in a forest flooded by spring runoff.*

"Then people were stopping. Somebody came over and took my dog, and I remember giving that person my wallet and telling him to take Guffy to a vet, and not to have the dog put to sleep. So Guffy was taken away while I lay there waiting for an ambulance. In the other car, a little girl was killed and the mother was paralyzed for life . . ."

There are good and honest strangers in this world. The next day, T.J.'s wallet was returned to him in the hospital—and shortly after that, a veterinarian called. Bad news: it would be best to simply put Guffy down. If the dog did live, there was no way he could ever be the same again. What was left wasn't worth saving. But T.J. was adamant: "No! Don't put my dog down! Do the best you can with him. But don't put him to sleep!"

T.J. was supposed to spend six weeks in the hospital; he checked out after only three. His father had flown down from Oregon, and together they went out to the vet clinic to get Guffy. It was a sight T.J. would never forget: "My dog was lying there looking like death warmed over. Shaved from the middle of his torso all the way back, and a mass of stitches where they had operated. The head of the broken femur had been smashed so badly that they simply cut it off and the

femur was no longer connected to the hip. There was that crushed pelvis, too, and some broken ribs."

Still—the dog was alive.

T.J. and Guffy went home to Oregon for Christmas and New Year's and then, badly crippled, they returned to Nilo and began the long road back. Through the rest of that winter the healing went on—T.J. on crutches and his dog limping painfully beside him. Spring came, and we would see them walking slowly down to a Nilo pond for the water work that was balm for Guffy's maimed hindparts. T.J. was on a cane by then, and Guffy was able to run after a fashion. Slowly, through late winter and into spring and summer, dog and master mended—working and learning, and talking together as they always had.

Just to stay alive, it was necessary for Guffy to exercise every day and stay in the best physical condition possible.

"It had to be done," T.J. explains. "The only thing that kept Guffy's hind leg in place was a mass of hard muscle; there was no bone connection with the hip." When T.J. wasn't working his dog afield, Debby would take

A flooded rice field is no match for the raw power of a chocolate Lab.

Guffy with her as she jogged. From the beginning, the young dog's agonizing rehabilitation was a bond of faith with T.J. and Debby. The simple act of standing was a triumph. From there he would learn to walk again and then, finally, to even run in a strange, shambling way.

The dog walked funny, sat funny, and was becoming arthritic. "He ran different," T.J. says. "His bad back leg wasn't quite in sync with the rest of his body. It slowed him down. Before the accident he was just running hard all the time; being crippled slowed him, and it may have made him think a little bit more . . ."

But the things that count most hadn't changed—the heart, the brain, and the steady, honest consistency with which a fine retriever serves himself and his master.

And just three years after the accident that crippled him for life, Guffy became the new national champion.

In 1979 some 5,000 retrievers tried to qualify for the National Championship Stake. Only 71 got there. Guffy would be among them.

The trial began on a crisp November morning near Redding, California, and Guffy ruled the field from the start. The tenth and last

Although the day is drawing to a close, this yellow Lab still hopes for one final retrieve before heading home.

Two hunters open fire with their Lab ready to retrieve any downed birds.

series of competition had been one of the toughest—a difficult qua-
druple water retrieve. Guffy was the first dog to run that final series. As
T.J. waited in the holding blind, the tension was almost unbearable. Up
to that point Guffy had worked beautifully. But could he keep up the
pace?

He could, and did. The dog seemed to think his way through that
final test and needed no handling at all. He was judged "excellent," just
as he had been in six of the 10 series of competition. (Only one other
dog would score "excellent" in the last series, and that was Paladin
VII—Guffy's brother.)

Guffy's triumph, T.J. has always said, belonged more to the dog than
the master. I was once asked what I thought when people called Guffy
a 'natural dog.' My answer was simply that his achievements belong
mostly to him and not to his handler or the methods of training . . ."

The new champion would lead a good life, and a long one. He was
nearly 15 years old when he died in February 1988, a beloved family
member until the end. But for all the gifts bestowed on such a dog by
the Red Gods, others may be withheld. From Guffy's national championship onward, he would sire no puppies—a sterility that may have
resulted from the terrible injuries three years before.

T.J. will never forget the grueling field trial campaigns, of course.
The victories, the trophies. The applause and honors. But through it all,
one of the things he remembers best was how Guffy would look at
him. Walking at heel, sitting beside him, or just lying at T.J.'s feet at day's
end, the great dog would watch his master's face with unblinking love
and trust. Here I am, boss. Ready when you are. What are we gonna do
next?

Way to go, Guffy. Good boy! Fetch 'em up!

OVERLEAF:
*Hunter and Lab rest in the frosty
sunshine for just a moment before
returning to the hunt.*

PASSAGES

by E. Donnall Thomas, Jr.

All Labs slow down with age, seemingly losing some of the powerful flushing and retrieving talent they have exhibited since adolescence. But the nature of the Lab drives him to hunt, and even the eldest of Labs will occasionally exhibit brilliant behavior in the field. These Labs are champions, as well.

A Montana physician and writer, E. Donnall Thomas, Jr. is a lifelong outdoorsman who has spent countless hours afield with Labs. He serves as the hunting editor for *Traditional Bowhunter* and contributes regular articles on bowhunting, wingshooting, fly-fishing, and wildlife to *Gray's Sporting Journal, Alaska, Shooting Sportsman, Sports Afield, Ducks Unlimited,* and *Retriever Journal,* among others. Thomas is also the author of nine books, including *Fool Hen Blues: Retrievers & Shotguns, and the Birds of the American West.*

A sleek pair of black Labs pauses for portraits after several energetic retrieves.

FROM THE PHYSICAL standpoint, Sonny conceded his primacy in the kennel back in October. Jake began his first season full of the unbridled puppy enthusiasm wild roosters love to exploit, bumping birds we should have killed and letting Sonny's seasoned guile make him look every inch the beginner in comparison. But after several weeks and lots of birds he began to settle down and learn from his mistakes, and I could tell that we had another solid bird dog in the making.

Then one hot Indian summer afternoon we parked the truck and watched a dozen roosters flush wild and sail into a swampy hell-hole choked with cattails and brambles as if they were daring us—us, the A-team!—to follow them into the heart of their turf. I knew there were easier birds waiting somewhere along the edges of the stubble, but letting pheasants dis you without responding has always impressed me as equivalent to the beginning of the end. I exchanged my hiking boots for my hip waders and let the dogs boil out of the back of the rig while Lori and my folks took up positions along the edge of the nastiness. Then the dogs and I waded in.

From the standpoint of locomotion, the cover turned out to be about as bad as it gets. All I could do was hold my shotgun overhead in one hand with the muzzle pointed safely at the sky and bull my way forward through the briars and the muck. The stuff seemed even harder on the dogs, who had to bounce up and down through the tightly woven cattails investing three feet of wasted up and down motion for every foot of genuine progress. The process proved exhausting, and by the time we reached the middle of the pocket, Sonny had returned to my side wearing a look of dismay and panting furiously.

Sonny was ten years old, and he carried more miles of hard hunting on his chassis than most working Labs will ever have the pleasure of knowing. During a decade of western pheasant hunting, his relentless tenacity had always (well, almost always) compensated for his faults. Now he stood there before me with his eyes closed as if he needed to concentrate on the business of panting, and when I finally got him to look at me the expression on his face reminded me of the way I felt when I packed a large bull elk out of the hills by myself the month before. In our own way, each of us had come face to face with the realization that there were certain things we just couldn't do anymore.

A dozen yards farther into the cover, we came to a stagnant lick of dog water. Sonny promptly threw himself into the mud to wallow like a pig and I held up to let him cool off and rest. In the meantime, I could still hear Jake crashing forward somewhere ahead of us, and then he had a rooster in the air. As a report from my father's shotgun interrupted the bird's angry cackle, a handful of feathers drifted back over our heads on the prairie breeze. Sonny rose to his feet at the sound of the shot but that was as far as he chose to take his participation. Jake made the retrieve unassisted.

A passage had taken place down in the guts of the cover. Sonny wasn't the undisputed top dog anymore.

Frost and fog don't dampen the spirits of this hunting black Lab at the ready.

A thick-necked and muscled hunting yellow Lab.

As the season wore on and Jake accounted for an ever increasing share of the birds we killed, Sonny regressed into a flaky canine second adolescence. He's always enjoyed the run of the place, but he began showing up at a neighbor's house two miles away at dinner time to bargain his charm for table scraps and we had to confine him to the house. He quickly learned how to open the doors and took to letting himself in and out at will, leaving the house exposed to freezing November temperatures. We had no choice but to remove him to the kennel proper, breaking the kids' hearts and leaving a bit of a dent in mine as well. When we hunted, he conceded the heavy cover to Jake with what I interpreted as petulance, and I had to wonder if a long, distinguished career was coming to a close right before my eyes.

But despite the fact that he was covering less and less ground, he still displayed an uncanny knack for being in the right place at the right time, and when we had a really tough retrieve to sort out, Sonny always seemed to be the one to get the job done. Because I had convinced myself that his best years were behind us, I frankly attributed most of these successes to luck.

I should have known better.

Winter: the tail end of life to Shakespeare, the tail end of the season to a pheasant hunter. The Christmas decorations have been up on Main Street for nearly two weeks and even though the kids are growing older just like the rest of us, they are getting the holiday twitches as surely as an eager dog on the trail of a running rooster. The weather has turned from pleasantly brisk to seriously cold and one can make a good argument for observing the relentless conclusion to the march of the seasons from indoors, in front of a loading bench, a fly-tying vise, or a fireplace.

But none of us is that old, not even Sonny. When I arrive at the kennel wearing hunting clothes he greets me with familiar enthusiasm, and the congenial mood expands when I invite him to join me in the pickup's cab. There is no whining from Jake back in the dog box, for I have already decided that today it will be just the two of us. We have issues, as a therapist might put it, and they are the kind of issues that can only be worked out one on one.

I have chosen to hunt a patch of river bottom habitat that both of us know well, enforcing the feeling that we are doing this for old times' sake. The cover ranges from placid to nasty, which will allow me to temper the hunt according to the old dog's endurance. By this time of year, there are always plenty of birds in the freezer, so it is an easy matter to subordinate the bag to the process. And that is how it should be, for I have not come today to

Still spry in the legs, a black Lab gracefully clears a downed tree.

shoot a limit of pheasants. I have come to renew a friendship.

The air above the river feels crisp and refreshing. Snow lies in strata underfoot: a crunchy layer of frozen sugar topped off by an inch of new powder. There are no bird tracks along the edges of the fields as we drive in, and I decide to begin with a push through the heart of the cover. The pheasants have been educated by two months of open season, and I do not imagine for a moment that any of them are going to be easy.

Hunting alone, the chance of flushing anything from the dense warren of brush beneath the cottonwoods seems minimal. We begin by walking in along the river, to isolate a patch of cover as effectively as possible and work it back toward a series of brush strips leading to the abandoned stubble fields. That is the kind of cover that will sometimes let even a seasoned rooster make a fatal mistake, and today I have the feeling we will need all the help we can get no matter how well Sonny performs.

The first half hour of the hunt is little more than a walk through the woods. Every time I have to push my way through a patch of brush, fresh snow cascades from the branches and down the back of my collar, but even the cold slick of melting snow against my skin can't compromise the relaxing pace of the day. There are no birds in the air, but there are tracks underfoot: coyotes, foxes, whitetail does, the old buck that eluded me during archery season, and finally a scattering of pheasants. Up ahead, Sonny is hunting steadily, as if the brisk weather and Jake's absence have retracted a few years from the calendar. All this is more or less what I had in mind. But as we continue our advance, I find myself thinking less about philosophy and more about the sound of flushing roosters. After all, issues aside, this is still a pheasant hunt.

As we near the edge of the heavy cover, Sonny begins to work the ground intently, and the tracking snow soon confirms to my eyes what his nose has already told him. There are birds running out ahead of us. The chase soon leads us into a narrow finger of chest high scrub that offers the pheasants only one avenue of escape: straight ahead. Two months earlier the cover might have held them, allowing us to walk them up while the dog flushed them for a shot. But these birds have been there, done that. I can visualize the hunt's conclusion as inevitably as a train wreck in progress, with birds squirting wildly from the end of the brushy finger while we stand and watch their escape a hundred yards behind them.

When the leaves begin to change, thoughts of days afield fill the minds of hunter and his Labs.

Fortunately, Sonny has other things in mind. Twenty yards ahead, the strip of brush makes a sharp turn to the right, and suddenly the dog is tearing off across the snow along the hypotenuse of the triangle. This brilliant little maneuver traps what turns out to be a lone rooster between us. As the dog works his way back toward me, the cock recognizes his dilemma and flushes loudly. In an instinctive attempt to split the difference between his pursuers, the bird rises straight up into

the winter air, affording me a point-blank look at his brilliant copper breast feathers before he crumples at the sound of the shot. With the dead bird's dark plumage planted squarely in the fresh snow, the retrieve is an absolute no-brainer, but I do not choose to share this observation with Sonny.

Satisfying as the bird feels in my hand, it occurs to me that I have just witnessed something far more complicated than one dead pheasant. Sonny's performance illustrates a fundamental difference between the demands we place on flushing Labs and pure retrievers. Theoretically, a good handler should be able to train a good dog to make just about any retrieve. It doesn't always work out that way of course, but at any given level of training, differences in retrieving ability usually boil down to minor variations in marking ability, nose, and heart.

On the other hand, at the risk of offending some professional handler out there, I would suggest that there is no way anyone can really train a dog to do what Sonny did to this pheasant. I certainly won't pretend to claim the honor. All I did was take an eager dog, raise him in a way that made him want to make me happy, and give him ten years of non-stop, pedal-to-the-metal experience in the field. He figured the rest out for himself.

As we walk together across the snowy field back to the pickup, I consider what an intangible, irreplaceable commodity those years of experience represent. Suddenly I understand: this is the key to understanding the passages I witnessed earlier in the season. Sure, Jake can hunt circles around Sonny now, but athleticism counts for only so much out here in the field. Jake could not have begun to outfox the bird resting in my game vest. Not yet.

Then I remember the day it all started, back in the cattails. My

ABOVE: *Mallard, goose, slippers, or log, this yellow Lab will retrieve it for you.*
FACING PAGE: *A pair of black Labs waits as their hunter glasses for geese in the Rocky Mountain foothills.*

Two chocolate Labs seem to skip across the water's surface in pursuit of downed geese.

father is gracefully approaching eighty, an age when most hunters are content to rest on their laurels and recall great times from years gone by. But there he was. And hey, *he* was the guy who shot the pheasant!

In fact, the demanding outdoor life consists of a series of passages punctuated by intersecting lines of ability. I remember the time my father sat me down at the end of a long day and informed me solemnly that I had become a better hunter than he was, just as I remember the day hunting partner Ray Stalmaster and I watched our young sons run circles around us on the way to the top of a mountain deep in the wilds of Alaska. In each case, lines of ability had intersected. Passages had taken place, and it could not have been any other way.

And so it goes with Labs as well. Old dogs will not keep up with young dogs, but the good ones don't have to. End of discussion; issues resolved.

Back at the truck, Sonny hops up onto the seat beside me. Today, he knows his place is secure. We have ended one season together, but he knows there will be another. And so do I.

ABOVE: *The end of a day, the end of a hunt. But the sun will rise anew, as it always does, and hunter and Lab will spend many more days afield.*
OVERLEAF: *Retrieving a pheasant to hand.*

Part III

THE CONSUMMATE HUNTING DOG

"From her earliest puppy days, [my Lab Gypsy] would prick her ears and look about her at the sound of a gun. She will watch an aeroplane right across the sky, and if it fell, I feel that she would gallop to its fall to bring it to me."
—Eric Parker, *Best of Dogs*, 1949

LEFT: *Waterfowl or upland game, the versatile Labrador retriever can handle them all.*
ABOVE: *With a soft mouth gripping a mallard drake, a black Lab successfully returns from her retrieve.*

The Dog that Hunts Anything

by John Barsness

Humans have been hunting for perhaps two million years; Labrador retrievers, at least in the form they are known today, have only been going afield for the last century or so. Makes you wonder how wildfowlers before the twentieth century ever got any game, for today, the Labrador retriever is an indispensable part of the pursuit of just about any type of waterfowl or upland game.

John Barsness has hunted all kinds of game with Labrador retrievers for more than thirty years. The author of six books, including *Western Skies: Bird Hunting in the Rockies and on the Plains* and *Shotguns for Wingshooting*, Barsness is a Montana-based freelance writer specializing in hunting, guns, and the outdoors for magazines such as *Field & Stream, Gray's Sporting Journal, National Geographic, Outdoor Life, Sports Illustrated,* and *Sports Afield.* Today, he shares his home with a chocolate Lab named Keith and a Lab–English setter cross named Gideon.

"The Dog that Hunts Anything," which chronicles the pursuit of a cornucopia of upland game with a birdy Lab named Gillis, originally appeared in *Shooting Sportsman.*

Confidence radiating from every pore, a magnificent yellow Lab is ready for whatever the hunter has in store for him today.

WHEN MY FIRST Lab was six months old, we spent a weekend with some friends who had a parakeet. Before then the pup's ears went up when he saw robins in the yard, but there'd been nothing to indicate he would sit under a birdcage for 48 hours. After the first day we began to think of him as a piece of furniture with a moving tail. I don't know what the parakeet thought.

A month later he and I walked a fenceline near some buffalo berrybrush along the Missouri River. Suddenly Gillis stopped and poked his black nose between the two lowest strands of barbed wire, and I half-raised the pumpgun. When the sharptails went up I shot one, and Gillis ran down into the brush and brought it back, tilting his head while giving the grouse tender readjustment bites. Apparently this seemed as natural to him as sitting under a birdcage.

Over the next three months he learned that birds live in the brush, pushing sharptails and pheasants out of the buffaloberries and chokecherries and wild roses in the coulees of northeastern Montana. Then he learned that ducks and geese live on water. This revelation didn't seem to bother him one bit, but he always liked scaring the hell out of brush-birds best.

It wasn't until the next fall that he got to scare a sage grouse. These hadn't hatched well for a couple of years, so instead of walking across a dozen miles of sagebrush hoping to stumble across a few, we sat on a hill above a stock dam in the wild country near Fort Peck Reservoir. Gillis whined softly a few times while I read a book, telling me this was no way to hunt: We should either be beside the water, waiting for ducks, or Out There, running through the sage and prickly pear, trying to panic grouse. I told him he should learn to read.

The coulee was in shadow and the water of the stock dam turned to silver by the time I glimpsed white movement in the sagebrush above the dam. It could have been the belly of a whitetailed jackrabbit slowly hopping toward the water, but even in the shadowed distance it had the walk-rhythm of a big sage rooster, as stately and pompous as the head of the Rotary Club on his way to the podium. I'd also found tracks and the white curls of sage grouse droppings along the pond's shore earlier in the afternoon.

I pocketed my book, and we walked down, Gillis at heel. When I released him, he rushed forward through the sage and stood, almost pointing for a moment, before rushing again, circling the edge of the sagebrush. He lifted his nose and rushed one more time, and a big grouse unfolded from the earth and flew just over the tops of the sage. I was carrying a 20-gauge double, and the rooster was close enough for the cylinder barrel. When the rooster folded a smaller hen got up, the size of a pheasant, and that, too, went down a little further out. Gillis was already heading back with the big one, carrying it by the base of the neck, but paused to watch the second bird go down before bringing the rooster in when I called.

With the aid of a Kevlar canoe, a hunter and his Labs shove off in pursuit of waterfowl.

Sage grouse often hatch spottily in the sage desert, where they live, but that same year Hungarian partridge did well. Plenty of nesting cover grew in the rose coulees, and the wheat harvest was a good one. I wondered what Gillis would do with birds that neither lived in brush nor floated on water.

We jumped the first covey in late September toward evening, along the edge of a wheatfield. Huns like field-edge dips, feeding in the tall stubble and waste grain. When flushed they usually fly out over the field, or a grassy hilltop, gliding and landing and then peeping softly to regather. This covey chose the field route. I told Gillis to stay, and we watched the birds fly, a dozen buzzing particles against the prairie sky. The buzzing stopped just when they grew almost too small to see, as they set their wings and sailed onto the subtle roll of a stubbled ridge.

I wondered again how this would work and then started walking. Gillis looked at me for a moment, but he'd seen the birds and knew which way they'd flown. He angled ahead, across the wind, then turned and came back when he reached good modified-choke range. Once he jumped a jackrabbit and I had to call him back, but mostly we just walked across the stubble, him quartering in front of me as if he'd been doing it all his life.

When we started up the slight incline of the ridge, I edged down-wind of where I'd marked the Huns down. Gillis edged over, too, and at the end of one swing he stopped. He held his nose up and into the

FACING PAGE: *Labrador retrievers are such talented hunters that they just might be able to forego a hunting partner altogether and call in ducks, down the birds, and make the retrieve all by themselves.*

ABOVE: *The setting sun silhouettes a romping Lab bouncing across an early winter marsh.*

OVERLEAF: *Adrift in a flooded forest in search of ducks.*

wind, moving it as if trying to follow the flight of a butterfly. He followed the scent like a kayaker picking his way down a stair-step of rapids, pausing and darting and then pausing again until absolutely sure. Toward the top of the ridge his head went lower and he found the ground scent, and when the covey went up it was as if I'd followed one of the longest points in history.

A few years later dove season finally opened in Montana, and he went with me, either sitting by my folding stool under the green cottonwoods or accompanying me jump-shooting birds in the stubble. He didn't care, though like most dogs he could have used some dental floss on the feathers between his teeth.

Before the next bird season I moved to the mountains of western Montana. I spent opening weekend carrying furniture, but a few days later I drove up Rock Creek, turning up a side road until I could see a coulee with aspens and huckleberry brush across a small creek. We got out and crossed the creek, me on a log and Gillis in the water, then headed up an elk trail and around the curve of the hill. He was used to working 20 or 30 yards out, but as soon as we entered the aspens he

Pleading eyes beg for you to get it together and down some birds.

held 20 or 30 feet in front, just far enough to keep track of me as we hunted. As his nose went sideways and he paused, I already had the 20-gauge halfway to my shoulder when the ruffed grouse went up. It was only wing-tipped, but Gillis caught it as it hit the ground.

Gillis hunted until he was almost 14. By then he'd flushed and retrieved eight of the 10 upland birds in the state—spruce, blue, ruffed, sage, and sharptailed grouse, and Huns, pheasants, and doves. He never got a chance to retrieve a whitetailed ptarmigan, since there isn't an open season, and I didn't use him on Merriam's turkey, though I'm sure he would have put up an October flock and brought the fallen back. As near as I can figure he retrieved 15 varieties of duck, along with Canada geese and common snipe. He dove for wounded ducks like a seal after cod.

A happy moment after a successful hunt.

He couldn't hunt the steep ridges that last fall, but did fine for two or three miles on the flats, chasing Huns over wheat stubble or sage grouse along level ridges. On his last day of Hun hunting I killed two birds with one shot on the first covey rise. One bird fell dead, but the second was only wing-broken, and Gillis had to follow it out of the covey scent and across the gusty stubble before pouncing on the bird.

But the thing I remember best about that fall was a day along the Judith River. Indian summer held all through September, just the thing for old dogs. We hunted opening day of pheasant season, Gillis and Eileen and I, and found one rooster and a covey of Huns. By late morning Gillis was done in, and so was Eileen, so she decided to hike across Arnie's stubble fields to the pickup, taking the dog. I decided to make one last swing through some low-rose washes on the other side of the ranch road.

As I lay the double gun on the ground to cross the fence, I heard Eileen shouting and turned to see a gray-muzzled Labrador trotting toward me, a quarter-mile away. By the time he reached me he was really tired, so I gave up my last swing and followed Eileen.

She'd walked halfway back to the pickup, she said, when Gillis jumped a couple of mourning doves. She doesn't shoot doves, partly because they're so small (she prefers to hunt big things, like geese and moose) and partly because she can't hit them. So she and Gillis watched the doves fly, and Gillis gave her a look that very plainly asked why she was carrying a shotgun since she obviously wasn't going to use it. Then he turned and headed straight for me. By that age he was as deaf as a cottonwood log and never glanced toward her shouts, but he was damn well going to hunt with someone who'd shoot the birds he put up.

I've hunted over other dogs, of course, mostly Brittanies and springers, but also some English setters and golden retrievers, and a few not-so-common breeds, like a Viszla and a Boykin spaniel. Each found birds and each in its own way was a good all-around dog.

But perhaps the largest virtue of Labs, even more important than doing a reasonable job on almost any bird, is their ability to survive the most amateur trainer. Gillis was a gift from my ex-mother-in-law, an eight-week-old surprise that made me a dog trainer before I was ready. He turned out to be such a good upland dog that over the years several friends left their dogs at home, or in the dog box in the pickup when we went hunting. That's more a tribute to Labrador retrievers than to my training.

There have been other Labs, too, like Norm Strung's Chief, Bill Gallea's Ellie, Dale Spartas's Buck, and others whose names have been forgotten. Most have been black, some have been yellow, and a few chocolate. Some, like Gillis, were lean English-style dogs, able to cover the uplands all day long; others were built like small Angus bulls, so strong they put up a wake when they swam. But they all had three things in common: a hunting sense of anything that flew, an uncommon desire to please their masters, and an intelligence so uncanny that at times they seemed to be able to understand complex speech.

I remember a party where Gillis came over to get petted by me and a guest. After a half-minute or so I said, "Okay, go lie down in the corner and play with your ball." And he did just that. But don't believe me. Charley Waterman, not a Lab man, wrote of hunting with someone else's retriever. He ended up alone with the Labrador in some thick grouse cover, telling the dog what was needed. Whether the dog understood, Charley didn't know—but the dog did it.

Hungarian partridge are the only Montana bird on which I've found pointing dogs do a demonstrably better job than a Lab. Probably the same could be said of most quail. But put a Lab in tight pheasant cover, where I seem to find most pheasants these days, and few springers do better. A close-working Lab is also good on ruffed grouse. For someone who hunts every bird imaginable, when he can and not constantly, who trains irregularly and sometimes loses his temper, there is no better breed. I know pointing-dog owners who say a flushing dog gives no warning of nearby birds. Well, you can't walk through a field, double gun broken, and casually converse with a friend when hunting with a Lab. You must pay attention to the dog—but if you do, he'll tell you everything you need to know. I could tell by watching Gillis whether he was smelling coyote or porcupine, or even the difference

FACING PAGE: *The Labrador retriever is, without a doubt, the consummate hunting dog.*

between Hun and pheasant scent. And in plenty of time for the shot. Labs cannot cover country like the best pointing dogs, but then neither can most hunters.

I have a new Lab now, three years old. He's a brown, 95 pounds, a very different beast than Gillis. Instead of weaving through pheasant cover, he flattens it. Instead of patiently cornering pheasants and sharptails, he herds them my way. But when he first met a stubble field, he quartered up Hungarian partridge naturally, the same way Gillis did. So far he's put up and retrieved only a quarter of the kinds of birds Gillis did, but on ducks and geese he's better. He quivers when anything flies, and when I say his name he looks into my eyes and tries so hard to understand English that someday we'll have conversations about the ways of wind and birds.

And if they ever open penguin season, we'll be there.

FACING PAGE: *A chocolate Lab and a pintail drake.*
ABOVE: *A yellow Lab flushes a pheasant for a hunter.*

BEN

by Paul A. Curtis

Paul A. Curtis sought birds with numerous canine companions during his long career as a shooting expert, editor, and author. Curtis served as the shooting editor for *Field & Stream* for fifteen years and later served as the editor of the magazines *Game* and *National Sportsman*. He contributed countless hunting sketches to the sporting magazines of his day, and penned seven books on hunting, including the *Outdoorsman's Handbook* (1920), *American Game Shooting* (1927), and *The Highlander* (1937).

"Ben," which originally appeared in Curtis's 1938 book *Sportsmen All,* is the story of a multi-talented Scottish Lab memorable in the field not only to his owner but also to King George V.

A content black Lab pauses for a rest along a lakeshore during a hard day of hunting.

A THICK MIST rolled in from the Atlantic. It swathed the Goat Fell, mighty sentinel of Bute, as in a winding sheet.

I knew before hearing my host's judgment, as we raided the mysterious dishes under their covers on the hot plate, that there would be no grouse shooting upon the high moors that day. His proposal, however, seemed quite as good indeed; and after a week's tramping in the heather above Glen Rosa and along Corrie Dhu, following such intrepid leaders of dogdom as Brodic Castle Brigadier, champion of Scotland and Ulster, it came as a relief. We were to try the low ground for a mixed bag, crossing Arran afoot, with a couple of gillies in attendance, aiming to reach a certain farmhouse in time for tea, where, afterwards, a good flight of wood pigeon was expected.

Thus we started, about ten o'clock. The motor swung out through the park drive, where the water dripped from the rank growth of rhododendron, past the Standing Stanes—rugged monoliths erected by the prehistoric people of the Isles long before the Roman Legions set foot on Scotia—on through the great iron gates, symbols of the dignity within, and purred along the narrow road which wandered like a white ribbon through the hills to the west, where the surge of the sea rolled relentlessly against Arran's rugged shores.

The motor slowed down at a quaint little bridge of the red stone of the country, and crooked as a dog's leg, so made in the old days that the devil might not cross, though why a gentleman so crooked and ingenious himself could not navigate them, has never been explained. On the other side of it the gillies rose from the heather and doffed their caps, wishing us a good morning in the soft Highland tone that is like a benediction, and received our lunch basket and shell bags.

There were but six of us: two gillies to carry the game and a plentiful supply of cartridges; Bonnie, an indefatigable red cocker that accompanied his master everywhere; a great lumbering brute of a Labrador; my host and me. We crossed a meadow, from which some lapwings rose lazily, conscious of their protection under the law, and assailed a steep bracken-clad slope into which Bonnie dove with industrious zeal.

In a moment one was sodden with moisture to the tails of his jacket, in evidence that whatever happened it would not be dry sport, but the action was swift. Before I had gone five rods there was a disturbance in the bracken, and a woodcock fluttered away in front of me, to go down at the first crack. The great Labrador went after it on command and I watched him come floundering back through the low cover, head aloft, to disgorge the bird in the outstretched hand of the gillie. Meanwhile Bonnie pushed out a rabbit which fell to his master, and a moment later I rolled another down the hill. One does not mind a wetting midst such excitement.

Both Ben, the Labrador, and Bonnie were kept busy for the next two hours. Pushing through a grove of birches we bagged another cock, and at the report there was a sharp clatter of stiff wings, and some

A chocolate Lab paddles across a Montana stream.

pigeons dashed from cover, of which we took our toll. A couple of hares were collected in the open, and sundry hedgerow rabbits, as well as a brace of black game from off the edge of the corn. Then we came to a stretch of bog, where the fun was fast and furious, for some snipe were there; we accounted for several couple, at the expenditure of considerable ammunition, before we capped the morning with a brace of teal at the far end. Such is rough shooting on Arran.

Through all this I had time to develop an increasing admiration for big Ben—floundering up to his belly in the black bog where the snipe rose—retrieving hares and sundry rabbits, to say nothing of the teal and the black game. He had done nobly and with never a mistake. Staunch as a rock he stood at heel behind the gillie, until sent out with a wave of the hand and a soft word of command to do his stuff, picking up his quarry and coming promptly back with head and stern in the air, always at a gallop. Plainly Ben was a lucky dog, for he was doing the thing which he loved best.

As the sun came out it revealed a broad stretch of purple moor low on the edge of the sea. My host suggested that we work it, to add a few brace of grouse to the variegated bag, while our sodden garments dried upon us, before sitting down to a belated lunch. Some tourists cycling by on the shore road paused to watch the sport and we soon gave them action, as a large covey rose with a cackle of protest and winged it back to the mountains where they belonged. We took eight-and-a-half brace off that bit of moor before we reached our resting place beside a little monument which had been erected to commemorate the day when King Edward VII had lunched there on a similar shoot with the father of my host.

Whilst we took off our shoes and wrung the water from our stockings, the gillies dumped their game bags on the ground and their contents were laid out in orderly array. Thirty-six head we had, according to my game register, and the afternoon flight yet to come. When the lads had put it away again and, spreading out the lunch, had retired to the lee of a boulder to eat their own, the two dogs sat down to watch us, with slavering interest, from an orderly distance.

I quaffed a bracer from a horn cup, diluted with burn water, and waded into one of the most delicious dishes in the world—a cold grouse pie. Having appeased my appetite I looked up, and there was the polite Ben gazing at me with a pleading look in his dark eyes, while his huge maw of a mouth slobbered and drooled like a cataract. Really, it was too much to bear! I reached into the pie and picked out a toothsome bit, as he cocked his head on one side, tail awag in anticipation. Having deftly caught the offering, with a smack of the chops he sat back again on his haunches, eying his master furtively, in fear of a reprimand.

"A grand retriever that—and well behaved too," I observed.

"Yes," said His Grace, "he is well broken. Ben is probably the best one I have ever had, but nevertheless he caused me one of the most

This yellow Lab is young yet, but it won't be long before the pup will be much more interested in the scent of gamebirds than the taste of a pine cone.

ABOVE: *Practically galloping across a shallow stream, a yellow Lab pursues a retrieve.*

FACING PAGE: *Jet black except for radiant brown eyes, a Lab sits for a portrait while afield.*

embarrassing moments of my life. Perhaps his good behavior is an atonement, but I shall never live it down."

"What happened?" I asked, knowing from the twinkle in his eye as he smiled reminiscently at Ben, that behind it there was a story worth hearing. He crossed one brawny knee over the other and settled himself in the heather before he replied. The thin cry of a curlew came to us from the rim of the sea. My eyes rested on the soft blue of the water, where far out on the edge of nowhere the little dun sails of the herring fleet were visible. Beyond them again lay Ireland, but the haze was too thick to reveal it. Loading my briar, I waited in anticipation.

"We used to have a place in the Midlands where we spent the winter. We went there to escape the rigors of that season in Scotland, and while I shot, the family hunted with the local packs. There was good partridge and pheasant shooting in that country. One of my neighbors had a magnificent pheasant shoot, and once, some years ago, King George came to shoot with him. The owner had been to no end of trouble to provide the best of sport and when I was invited, naturally I accepted, and I took Ben, who was then a highly promising three-year-old, with me.

"We drew for position, which His Majesty always insisted upon, and it so happened that I was next to him in the first drive. As you know, His Majesty was a first-class shot—one of the best in the Empire—and absolutely deadly on high pheasants, but aside from that keepers have canny ways of their own of pushing the birds to that part

Five-of-a-kind ready for a day's hunt.

of the line where they know, from previous experience, the best guns will be. Naturally they want to have a big bag and one cannot prevent their doing it or blame them especially. So, despite the fact that there had been no favoritism, and he had drawn his peg with the rest of us for position, there was always an exceptional showing of birds over that part of the line where the King was posted, and, naturally, he had a lot of them about him when the whistle blew.

"Our friend Ben, over there, behaved splendidly, sitting behind my loader like a graven image until the drive was over, and retrieving my birds with dashing style, just as he did today. I was proud of him and confident in his behavior, so when he had collected my lot, I called him to heel and went over to the King's stand.

"'Sir,' I said, 'may I send out my dog to assist?'

"'Ah, thanks very much, Montrose,' he replied. 'Very kind of you.' So, as I said, full of confidence, I sent Ben out again and he behaved quite up to form, earning an approving comment from His Majesty.

"Well, to make a long story short, after lunch in the rotation of the stands I found myself again beside His Majesty, and we had a furious drive. The birds were coming over so high against a grey sky that they looked like sparrows, but time and again I observed that he had two dead in the air in front of him as he reached for his second gun. When the beaters came through to the edge of the woods and the feu de joie was over, Ben made my pick-up and I again joined the King.

Completely focused on the task at hand, a black Lab returns with a mallard drake.

A blue-eyed chocolate Lab pup chomps on a stick.

"'By jove, we have need for him this time,' he said, or words to that effect, and his eyes were sparkling. He had as many birds grassed behind him as he had in front, and Ben and his Clumbers were sent out further and further, bringing in the nearest first and then extending their range.

"It was a double drive, in which the guns remained in the same stands while the beaters went around and drove the birds back from the opposite direction, together with the undisturbed ones which occupied the woods, which became our new front. Under such conditions I made a mistake in sending Ben out so far, as he might easily have put back some birds near the edge, but he was doing splendidly until a winged bird, lying doggo in a clump of grass, got up in front of him and legged it for the cover, with the brute in hot pursuit. I blew my whistle like mad, but he disappeared in the woods—and then it happened!

"I heard him giving tongue frantically, while keepers cursed and shouted, and, to our utter amazement, hares broke from the woods in every direction, the majority of them dashing across our front, with that silly brute coursing as if he were in the Waterloo Cup, as he passed the King.

"Of course we were all disorganized—no one had a gun loaded—most of us, having finished the pick-up, were walking about smoking cigarettes with some neighbor when the Charge of the Light Brigade went through our batteries. There were a few scattered shots into the

rear guard that bowled over a couple, but almost everyone, save myself, was too paralyzed with laughter even to lift a gun."

His Grace paused reminiscently before he continued with a hint of reproach in his voice. "You know, my host was furious with me! Oh, quite!—in fact he never asked me over again—would hardly speak to me. It seemed that there were a lot of hares on his place and the head keeper had them driven into that woods the day before. Nets had been drawn about it with a lot of roots in the center to hold them. When the hares had been pushed in the opening, the nets were quietly closed, and there they were. It was hoped that it would provide a surprising diversion on the last drive and would have, too, if Ben had not landed in the middle of them just as the net was opened. I never really blamed him, poor chap; such a collection of hares scattering about like a bomb shell would be enough to put anyone off. Of course I never heard the end of it—hardly dared go near my club for a month.

"About a year later I was aboard the Admiral's flagship at Portsmouth when His Majesty reviewed the Fleet. We senior officers were drawn up on the quarter-deck when he was piped aboard. He walked slowly down the line, shaking hands with everyone, passed me with a word of recognition, and then bethought himself and turned back. With a gleam of amusement in his eyes he raised himself on his toes, with a hand cupped to his lips, and whispered into my ear, 'Oh, I say, Montrose, how *is* Ben?'"

When we reached the designated farm some hours later and had disposed of a formidable tea, which the farmer's wife had awaiting us, the light was already soft on the hills. Hurriedly we made off to a fine stand of firs surrounded by fields of yellowing corn, where the wary wood pigeons were expected to come to roost. As the gillies were going off to expedite matters by putting them up from near-by covers, I was placed at my stand with Ben for a companion. I was cautioned to let the birds come well in so that they would not drop in the corn, and if any did, on no account to let that lumbering brute go after them, as he would trample it down like a hippopotamus in a rice paddy. Ben sat down patiently beside me, as I loaded, and we prepared to wait.

The little world about us was busy in its quiet way, preparing for the night. Sheep bleated on the near-by hills, and from the slobs offshore the curlews were beginning to flight inland with plaintive cries, while their smaller brethren of the coast hustled complainingly about, gleaning the last bit of provender before the encroaching tide.

Silently a pigeon swept in overhead, and, spying us, swiftly changed direction with a diverting dive, but not too late to be intercepted. Ben retrieved it and I cleared his mouth of the feathers. There were several lots of pigeons now in the air, winging about at long range, as the walkers put them up. I shot a couple and missed as many more. Then came a lull. From somewhere near-by we heard the mellow COO-COO-COO of a bird that had slipped into the trees from in

FACING PAGE: *Three yellow Labs wait to get into the truck that will take them to the fields.*

A perfect day to hunt.

back, unaware of our presence, and Ben cocked his ears, while from a wee shealing on the brae above us came the soft strains of a lament, as some shepherd practiced upon his pipes. Then, on a sudden clatter of wings that roused us from daydreams, a flight of pigeons was all about us, and for a few moments I was busy loading and firing. There was a constant flow of birds towards the woods, and the more distant ones were not disturbed by the firing. When it was over I had several of them scattered about me, which Ben found with ease, but there were a few more out in the corn—where they had inadvertently fallen—and he knew it too. Ben started for it and with a vision of the irate farmer and my instructions, I called him back.

"No! Ben—aboo!"

Like a flash he put on the brakes and came back to heel. There was no doubt about it—that day when he ran amuck and mussed up the King's hare drive—Ben had been taught a never-to-be-forgotten lesson.

DUCKS AND THE WINGS OF DEATH

by Mel Ellis

Mel Ellis is one of the masters of outdoor writing, having penned hundreds of columns and articles over many years as the outdoors editor for the *Milwaukee Journal,* an associate editor for *Field & Stream,* a syndicated columnist for the Associated Press, and a freelance writer for dozens of national magazines. He also somehow found time to write more than twenty books, including *Ghost Dog of Killicut* (1969), *Wild Goose, Brother Goose* (1969), and *Flight of the White Wolf* (1970); the latter two were brought to the big screen by the Walt Disney Company. The winner of the Gordon MacQuarrie award for conservation writing, the Dorothy Canfield Fisher award and the Sequoyah award for children's literature, and the Audubon award, Ellis is simply one of the best.

"Ducks and the Wings of Death," which originally appeared in the November 1957 issue of *Field & Stream,* is a classic Ellis tale of a hunt in extreme conditions and a heroic Lab that is singularly focused on retrieving, no matter what obstacles he faces.

Ducks seem to rarely make an appearance in the most hospitable places. Often hunter and Lab must pursue waterfowl in wet, cold, windy, and sometimes even downright dangerous conditions.

The Strawberries are a Lake Michigan island group a few miles off Wisconsin's Door County peninsula. In November they deal in death and golden-eye ducks. There's little to tell about the young school-teacher and his wife and the others who died there, because only their boats and their bodies were left to bear witness. About the golden-eyes I can tell you.

Of all the ducks they come last, riding the winds when ice slicks the decks and the water is so much warmer than the air that the lake steams like a big kettle boiling. They come high and their whistling wings betray their presence even above the crashing of the waves on the slabstone shores. Called whistlers by some, they rocket from the sky at dawn and wing down the wave troughs, adept as pelicans. Then they smack to the water, and before the guns can get going they dive to feed. They die hard on the water and in the air, and there isn't a dog living that can swim down a cripple. They're beautiful and wary and there is something about them as wild as an Arctic storm.

Only one of the islands of the Strawberry group has a harbor sheltered enough to take a boat adequate for the trip from the mainland. So Capt. Les Anderson lowered me in darkness over the side a hundred yards from shore where whitecaps mark a reef. I stood waist-deep, waiting for the water to well up over my waders, and when it didn't I told the captain to hand me the bag of blocks. I floated them ashore and went back, marking by the running lights where the boat bobbed on the waves. This time he handed me my gun, a vacuum bottle of coffee, a bundle of sandwiches and an extra box of shells.

"The dog won't jump," he said as I turned and started shoreward again.

"Throw him in, then," I said.

I heard the splash. I whistled and kept walking, but when I was safe on shore Black Panther's Ace was not with me and the tiny boat lights were far out, visible at precise intervals as the craft plunged with the waves.

I whistled again, but the sound was washed right back at me by the breakers, and I knew that if the Lab didn't smell land he might swim until he went down. But he's a wise one, that dog, and by the time I had carried my gear to the lee point he was on shore, shaking.

My blind would have to be of stone to blend with its background; so I carried and rolled limestone slabs into position and then, when the sky turned gray, waded out to set the blocks. They moved with the waves until their anchors caught on the bottom, and then they turned to face the wind, diving through the crests and sideslipping in the troughs.

Even so, Lake Michigan was on her good behavior. If she took the notion to go on a rampage, half the island would be running with water as the waves smashed against the rocks, to go foaming across low land. "It's your funeral if she storms," Anderson had warned me.

This yellow Lab knows hunting is serious business.

But the previous morning the golden-eyes had worked the tiny outcropping on which I was now located, while we sat a mile away on the big island and got only occasional flurries of action. "Put me off over there," I had said, "when we come back tomorrow."

Anderson said he would if I was prepared to spend a night or several nights on the island. "Because if she blows," he explained, "there isn't much chance that I can get you off."

"I'll risk it," I said.

There was an old shack without windows or doors and minus one wall, but it would break a wind. There were skeleton-like trees, whitewashed to their death by the gulls, and they would furnish firewood. There was a lake full of drinking water. And there'd be the sandwiches and coffee, plus the ducks I planned on shooting. I had the dog for company, and I figured I could stick it out even until the lake froze a bridge to the shore.

The loyalty to Labrador retrievers of this hunting club is readily apparent in the name, Black Dog Hunting Club.

But it didn't look as though I'd have to, because the sun came up bright and the only clouds in the pale-blue sky hung low over the mainland near Fish Creek. A mile straight across, Anderson was in a blind of cedar, and though I couldn't see him or hear his gun I knew he and perhaps other gunners were shooting when a raft of golden-eyes got up on the wind and rode it straight down to me. They spotted the blocks, broke formation and skidded in and were feeding underwater even before I had the safety off. Ace started to go; so I grabbed him, hoping the ducks would swim within range. But they headed for open water and drifted away with the wind and the waves.

A big drake came whistling around the island and lowered his landing gear when he saw the decoys. The moment he put his flaps down full I pulled and he skidded dead into a breaking wave. The dog hurried, and then there was tonight's dinner beside me in the event Anderson failed to slide in close enough to take me off.

Three hens came in then just an inch above the spray, and two went down when I shot, but both dived and the dog had a pair of cripples to chase. I helped by getting a quick shot into one, but the other took the dog out where he couldn't hear the whistle and where his head looked like a cork among the waves. He must have lost sight of the duck, because he came back. And that was good; there wasn't a chance he'd ever swim it down, and if a fog front moved in he'd have some trouble in getting back. Now there were two ducks, more than I could eat, and if it wanted to storm I didn't care. It does a man good sometimes to have to slug it out with the elements—if for no other reason than to heighten his appreciation of the comforts surrounding him at home.

I didn't notice the wind shifting until the sound of shooting reached me. My companion on the big island was into a flock, and though I hadn't heard his gun all morning I could hear it now because the wind had swung around to the north and was carrying the sound to me. It had increased in velocity, but the sky was still blue and the only clouds were thin, shredded wisps high and wind-torn.

The change in the wind washed the blocks ashore and tossed them onto the island. I killed one final golden-eye as the last decoy rattled among the rocks, and then the dog was in trouble trying to make land with the duck. The breakers picked him up and hurled him to land, and each time he scrambled for footing on the moss-covered rocks the backwash sucked him out into the lake again.

If a wave should dash him against one of the protruding boulders, he'd be lucky to escape with only a few broken ribs. But he kept the

Hunter and Lab take a quick break during a duck hunt in an Arkansas marsh.

Icy conditions won't dampen the will to hunt for seasoned hunters and Labs.

duck and I could see it was a big drake with a white cheek and a crest as purple as a mountain in shadows. I could even see the pure gold of its eye as I waded as far as I dared and waited for the dog to ride another wave toward shore.

He came catapulting on a breaker, and I dug my fingers into his scruff as he swept abreast. Then we both braced as the waves sucked at us like some living tentacled thing intent on dragging a victim to a deep lair. The pain was all in my fingers and the dog's head went under water, but when the pressure was off Ace dug in and, like the big black cat he is named for, the Panther dog clawed his way across the rocks and up the shore.

The blind was awash when I got back to it, and my sandwiches were a speck of white that I could hardly discern, since the package was headed south among the foam flecks. One duck had disappeared. The thermos had smashed. The other duck was wedged between two rocks, threatening to become dislodged at each watery assault. The gun was under water; so I moved it first.

Then I went back, but the duck was gone, and I couldn't find any of the shells that had been standing in a box in the corner of the blind. I took stock on the knoll where Ace lay beside the drake. I had one duck, half a dozen shells and thirteen wet matches. Very carefully I put the matches in the corner of the old building beneath a board. I'd dry them in the wind and then open a shell and start my fire with gunpowder.

It was important that I dry my clothes. So I stripped to my under-
wear, put the wet waders back on, and tied my trousers, shirt, socks and
jacket in the wind. The sky was still clear, but the temperature was
tumbling. The clothes froze before drying. So I put them back on,
pulled on the wet waders and was warm enough.

I was inspecting my matches when I heard the boat whistle. I ran
to the shore and there she was, a hundred yards out, tossing so that I
could get but brief glimpses of Anderson standing at the wheel. He
waved several times, then swung
the boat directly into the wind
and pulled away. I watched until
there was nothing but a thin
thread of smoke, and went back
to make camp for the night.

Like my clothes, the matches
had frozen before drying. I tried
one and it crumbled. I warmed
another in my hand until it
thawed and then held it in the
wind to dry. Tentatively I
scratched it against a small stone,
but it broke to pieces.

Ace had bedded down. He
slept curled against the wall. The
wind trembled the wall. The wall
trembled the dog. But he slept
regardless. I looked at the

golden-eye. Its white breast was the only bright thing in the shack. The
walls were on the verge of crumbling anyway. Perhaps this was the
wind that would do it.

*A look of "What were you thinking
sending me out in this weather?"
emanates from this Lab.*

Well, I wasn't hungry, and the wind would probably die down,
come evening. Then Anderson might come back. Meanwhile I'd walk
and keep warm enough to get my clothes to dry on me. Water was
running over the south and north points of the island. Gulls huddled
on the rocks and on the bleached driftwood in the middle of the island.
They lifted a few feet when I approached and hung fluttering like
white rags in the wind, then drifted right or left to settle back,
hunkering down close to the earth.

Across the island I could see what also looked like a gull flopping
helplessly a few feet from the ground. It was a gull long dead, strangled
in the fork of a ground-hemlock branch that also had long since died,
suffocated beneath gull whitewash. The bird was nothing but bones and
feathers—a rather sharp reminder of what remains when an island traps
a man.

Here, tight to the shore, was half an acre of relatively calm water.
No place to bring a boat but refuge for a hundred golden-eyes and a
few mergansers and buffleheads. As I approached they crowded to the
far edge of the oasis of calm, then lifted in a cloud when Ace came up.

The flock turned on the wind and frantically beat its way back to the calm water.

The wind was a tumultuous thing now. It was carrying brush, howling through the high rocks, whipping foam off the breakers and casting it like snow. The little island was swallowed by sound, held by sound, crushed by sound. I talked to the dog, but he didn't perk his ears because the wind took my words and he didn't hear them.

I reached over to touch his head and he lifted his tail but didn't wag it.

This, I thought, was why hardly anyone availed himself of the golden-eye shooting on the Strawberries in November. This was the reason the islands often offered such secluded and spectacular shooting. Now I knew why few men ventured to them in small boats. This was what must have killed the young schoolteacher and his wife. Snow on this wind could kill me—now, later tonight, tomorrow or perhaps the following day.

But the sky was still clear. And the waders kept out the wind and kept in the heat. And as long as I stayed put there was no danger. Those who died here probably did so when they tried to run for it. I couldn't run if I wanted to. I had to sit tight, sweat it out, keep warm, try to build a fire so that I could roast my duck, because I'd have to be nearly starved before I'd eat it raw. Golden-eyes, though beautiful and sporting ducks to hunt, are not much of a table fowl. Their diet of crayfish, mollusks, crustaceans and fish sometimes makes their flesh stringy and strong.

FACING PAGE: *Don't let the general aura of cuteness fool you: This Lab has a heart devoted to the hunt.*
ABOVE: *A black Lab waits for the hunter to catch up.*
OVERLEAF: *A chocolate Lab in a lake under more favorable conditions.*

I wondered if this was the island where the young couple had been hunting, or the two high-school boys or the old man. It would seem so, because the other islands of the group had shelters in which they might have waited out a storm. No one would ever know, of course, any more than anyone would ever know exactly how they died.

Far out another flock of golden-eyes were trying to come upwind to the half acre of calm. It was easy to understand now why wildlife artists like to put this species on canvas. The flock, almost motionless in the air, was an etching in black and white against the pale sky.

There were the decoys to collect; so I went back to the north point but found only one. Its anchor string was caught in a bush. The others had evidently been sucked back by the lake or blown away by the wind.

It occurred to me that I ought to shoot a few ducks while they

were ganged up in the lee—just in case. At the shack I took two shells. On the shore I decided on a pair apart. I shot and both ducks dived. I never saw them again. I waited until a single detached itself from the big flock. When its neck was craned I shot again, hoping a pellet would get it in the head. The duck flopped about. The rest of the flock lifted and moved downwind. Ace bounded into the water, but just before he got to the duck it dived and didn't come up again until it was far out where the waves were running. I shouted for the dog and he came, without urging, up out of the icy water, glad to be ashore.

I couldn't risk another shell now. Not that there was any danger, nothing serious—unless the clouds came building black castles along the horizon. I thought about sleeping, curling up behind the walls of the shack. But in this tumult? With the wind running riot? And with the temperature still dropping?

The waves were throwing ice now. The ice clung where the spray wet the brush. It slicked the rocks. It whitened the dog's whiskers. At this time of the year subzero temperatures were not uncommon. That could mean trouble—if I slept. So we walked, that black dog and I, in a tight circle between the white gulls, which lifted out of our way and settled back again, feathers compressed tightly, beaks straight into the

A troika of black Labs.

wind. We walked and I talked to the dog the way I do when we're alone, but the dog didn't hear me. I could hear myself, though, and that mattered out here on this tiny island in the wind.

We walked for an hour, and I was as tired as if I'd walked for ten. The wind sucked strength right from the marrow of a man. It drained a man. It numbed him. I went back to the standing walls of the shack. I tried a match. It crumbled. I rubbed one gently in my hair. It sparked, but went out.

I'd get fire from one, I knew. So I whittled splinters and built a tepee of slivers. Then I tried another match in my hair. I rubbed gently, patiently—a long, careful while. This time the spark lighted the match. The flame was colorless until it began eating splinters. It hurried to the tip of the tepee and my fire burned.

I had hardly heaped on boards and had the fire roaring at a comforting warmth when I was startled by a thin, distant sound I couldn't place. It kept repeating, near, then far, as the wind tossed it. I turned, and there bobbed the boat a hundred yards out like a huge gull on the wild water.

A chocolate Lab leaps into a lake for the retrieve.

I ran to the shore and waved. When the boat hit a crest, I could see Anderson wave. There were others too, and they were putting a skiff over the side and I wondered what they meant to do. The boat tossed and was swept away. In a few seconds it was nearly ashore. But just before striking the outcropping rocks she swung her bow into the wind and held. Then I saw the hawser lift clear of the water, slap back into the waves, and I knew what they wanted me to do.

They wanted me to run for it, and that's when you get hurt. But I went for my gun, took one long look at the bright, warm fire and went back to the beach. The breakers poured water over my waders and slapped foam in my face. The stern of the boat came up and caught me so sharply under the chin that I was dazed. I threw myself forward and scrambled to the bottom of the skiff and hung on.

Then I remembered the dog, and how he'd never be able to get aboard, but when I raised up he was on his way back to the shelter of the shack and I cursed him proper. They had started pulling in the skiff, and I shouted for the dog to come, even though I knew he couldn't hear me.

In a way I couldn't blame him for preferring the fire and the shelter of the three walls to the open skiff bucking the waves like a thing gone berserk. He'd be all right if he didn't try to come off. You didn't get

hurt if you didn't run. He could eat the duck and the bones of the dead gulls, and when things quieted we could take him off.

I raised on an elbow during a comparative lull and there was my dog. He had gone back for the duck and was swimming with it toward the skiff. So I scrambled to the stern and lay low waiting, and when he lifted alongside I rose up and grabbed his tail and his scruff and yanked him aboard.

Then we lay low like two ants on a curly leaf. The water in the boat deepened. The bow took more decisive plunges with the added weight. The skiff rode more awkwardly down the troughs and climbed the crests laboriously. But it was a short pull, and the sides of the big boat loomed and dipped and fell alongside us.

As the craft bumped, hands came over the side and the dog disappeared. I got to my knees. The hands came down again and I leaped and was over the side and floundering on the icy deck like a big fish, wet and cold and exhausted.

After a few seconds I got to my feet and grabbed the rail. Before stumbling into the warm cabin I looked at the shack, ablaze on the island—the island where golden-eyes come in bleak November on icy winds, the island where a man can die hunting such harmless creatures as ducks.

FACING PAGE: *A chocolate Lab hunting in early winter in the American West.*
ABOVE: *A yellow Lab retrieving a duck.*
OVERLEAF: *Time to head for home.*

Part IV

OLD FRIENDS AFIELD

*"I think the bond between dog and man is
stronger in the retriever breeds than in any of the
other hunting dogs because of the basic requirement
of the teamwork necessary to get the job done."*
—Richard A. Wolters, *Water Dog*, 1964

LEFT: *The few days every year that hunters and Labs get to
spend afield eventually collect into a lifetime of wonderful
memories.*
ABOVE: *A young chocolate Lab with a long life of hunting
ahead of her relaxes on top of a muskrat lodge.*

GRAY MUZZLES

by John R. Wright

The passage of time affects us all, canine and human alike—everything gets a little creakier, a little slower, and a little grayer. But the desire to pursue game does not change in hunter or Lab, and year after year the two old friends will head for the marshes with decoys and shotgun in search of ducks.

John R. Wright and his Lab Peach know this passion for waterfowling and ultimately spent some fourteen seasons hunting together. Wright is a jack-of-all-trades, employed variously in his life as a carpenter, cartoonist, big game hunting guide, and camp cook. He is also a writer—the author of *Trout on a Stick* (1991) and the scribe of numerous articles for *Ducks Unlimited, Gun Dog,* and the *Retriever Journal.*

"Gray Muzzles" originally appeared in the May/June 1994 issue of *Ducks Unlimited.*

Years of experience under his collar, a yellow Lab pauses along the banks of a western river.

FOR THE FOURTH time since turning in, I raise up to check the glowing clock face. It is finally 4 A.M. and time to roll out. I swing my legs over the edge of the bed and the dog hears the springs complain. She pulls herself up with effort. She's wanted one of those L.L. Bean cedar dog beds for years, but the old couch cushion with a quilt over it seems to satisfy.

She passes me on the stairs as we go down, her joints all a-pop. Neither of our bladders is what it used to be, so she is as happy to be let out as I am to get to the bathroom. By the time I have the coffee started, she asks to come back in.

We're going out for ducks today, like so many times before. I've been a hunter for more than 30 years. She was born one. She'll be nine her next birthday, and I'll be 46.

Peach, named for the shade of her yellow Lab's coat, goes back upstairs for a few more winks before we head out. The dekes are already in the truck and the ancient, patched waders hang warming by the woodstove. Things were checked through and laid out last night, so I need little time to locate calls, whistle, shells, and fowling piece. But it does take awhile, at that.

The squashed disk in my neck is making itself known this morning, sending waves of dull pain down my right shoulder and arm. The recoil of magnum duck loads won't go unnoticed today. Then there are the less insistent naggings from knees, elbows, and other parts, all eager to remind me that football does, indeed, build character. Peach is not without her miseries, either. She seems to be a touch arthritic this season, packing her right rear leg at times, sitting with it shot out straight, and generally trying to keep her weight off it.

The coffee's ready and after an eye-opening, scalding slug, I return to the bathroom and the medicine cabinet to fetch an aspirin for the dog. She patiently accepts her pill by way of my finger poked down her throat.

I start the truck, then come back in to finish the coffee. My back is starting to loosen up and by now I can bend over enough to duct-tape my socks to my pant legs. If I fail to do this, the socks will be wadded into the toes of my wader boots before I've gone 50 feet. Peach hears the truck running and comes back downstairs. She, too, is moving a little easier and reminds me that she's ready for breakfast.

Outside, I drop the tailgate and open the door of her dog box. She waits politely for the command "load up." Her jump is good, but for that bad leg, which trails a bit behind. I'm standing by and give her just a little push—she would have made it anyway. In the cab I run my checklist once more. Decoys, calls, whistle, license, half a box of steel number ones, and the old double.

Ten minutes from home is the all-night market where I stop to fill my go mug. Somehow, their coffee is always better than mine. I get a couple of doughnuts I hardly need and nuke them a little in the microwave. Hunter and dog are better larded this season than last. I

Hunting in a late autumn snowstorm.

draw a stare from the wormy-looking graveyard clerk. I guess it's the lanyard and calls around my neck. Them's my "bonafidees," I think to myself. Man's gotta have proof of a good reason to be out and about this early. Don't want to look like some drunk who hasn't gotten to bed yet.

Back at the truck, I push a last bit of doughnut through the grill of the dog box door and watch it vanish. This produces a series of tail thumps against crate sides.

It's black as the inside of a bull when we get to the reservoir. I'm always early or late. The engine runs, the heater blows, and I drink more coffee, intimidated by the thought of setting out blocks in the waist-deep water. The small, persistent leak in the crotch of my waders remains unfound and so unrepaired. There's nothing but country on the radio at 5:45 A.M. and I finish the coffee as some unidentified down-home crooner laments his misspent youth. You and me both, Bubba.

The faintest dab of pink in the east spurs me to action. The dog jumps stiffly to the ground, but

Memories in the making: A chocolate Lab, a boat, a reedy marsh, and, somewhere nearby, ducks.

limbers up fast and is soon rolling on her back in the snow. While I heft decoys, bird vest, and gun, Peach rushes into the remaining blackness like the pup that still rules her heart. She checks back shortly before I reach the lake's edge and I heel her up to keep her out of the water. Her habit of swimming out with me as I set the decoys is too taxing for her these days. Better to spare that bone-wracking chill for honest retrieving.

One of the dekes has a massive fissure in its belly, so 11 will have to do. By then, I feel the magic fingers of ice water tickling at my nether regions and I'm very anxious to make landfall. My bird vest goes down in the cattails for the dog to sit on as I arrange spare shells and break off stalks that might impede my swing. No blind here, just the old "hunker down in the weeds" routine. Then I stand and wait for daylight. I have found that legal shooting time and enough illumination for the dog to mark usually arrive at about the same pace.

It's brightening fast now and I load up. The dog's ears rise at the snap of the closing action and again as I tune up on the call. No slowing of the blood there. Her anticipation is as strong now as in her first season. Mine too.

I'm cold, though, and it occurs to me that a certain amount of toughness has been lost over the years. Seldom anymore do I undertake the long, wet belly crawl to jump maybe one bird that was standard operating procedure a few seasons back. The great need to shoot the gun and fill the bag has drawn away some and simply being here takes on new dimensions. But for the dog to work, which has become everything for both of us, the odd duck must be killed and, as if summoned by that thought, a bluebill sizzles by at Mach-2 with me standing tall and flat-footed. Raising the gun from a very relaxed port arms I mount it, release the safety, socket the butt into that shooter's sweet spot, swing hard, and in one oily smooth motion, shoot at least four feet behind the bird. Peach watches the duck, looking for a hitch or a wobble, but ultimately has no reason to leave her seat.

Birds are in the air now, and I kneel in the snowy cattails, recharge the right barrel, and send out a hail call to whom it may concern. My knees are soon a pair of burning pincushions, part from the cold and part from the reluctance to bend. So much has been left on the playing field. A glance at the dog tells me she feels it too, that suspect leg extended out from under her weight. And so it goes for the next hour. Another pass by. Another miss.

I am contemplating an organized retreat when that absolutely gripping sound comes to us from above and behind—wind slicing

Many beautiful days afield lie ahead for these two young hunting partners.

through pinion feathers—and I hunch down and crane my neck to see two drakes with bottle-green heads drop and turn out past the far edge of the stool, coming about into the wind and across the gun at 60 yards. I wait and fight to stay still, my heart doing that trip-hammer jig it learned long ago. As the birds cup wings and toe up to that invisible dead-certain mark, I get an instantaneous and totally dominating cramp in my right hip causing me to lurch and come to my feet as if on strings. The birds flare at 40 yards, towering rapidly and putting distance between us.

Then in a slow-motion reversal of fortune, things begin to work. The pain fades as the gun lifts itself and tracks the high bird, tracing its bead along the stretched green neck, going past and building daylight. Swinging harder still, I pull the back trigger for the choke barrel. The kick is not felt, the report not heard, but I see the drake tumble and the dog go, both casting up diamond slivers of skim ice as they hit the water together.

He's a cripple, leading the dog on a merry chase out beyond the ice rim. At 75 yards she finally dives with him, going under head and all. When she gets back she's winded, but has the duck and delivers to hand.

As always, she is very proud of herself and well she should be. She has broken through ice and fought her way to clear sailing. She has gone round and round with a diving cripple and done what all dogs hate—gotten her ears full of ice water on her subsurface retrieve. She has done a smashing good job and she knows it, jumping straight up and down as I praise her, pet her, and admire the duck.

A black Lab retrieves a mallard drake.

A little break from a training session for some aggressive belly scratching.

It's a nice fat bird and she wants to worry it a little. I sack it and rub her up with the decoy bag. She likes it and thanks me with "that look." We confer and decide we're unlikely to top my shot or her retrieve, so we decide to go to the house. Peach is happy, knowing that when she is wet and it's just the two of us, she gets to ride back in the cab with me.

At the cabin again she gets another aspirin and I get the whiskey jug down. She curls up behind the woodstove as I toss in a chunk. Soon she is twitching in dreams I wish I could see. Her face has turned almost completely white now and, wiping my mustache, I realize mine has too. But the marsh was made for two gray muzzles like us. And you know what? After our nap, there's the evening flight.

After a day of hunting, backed up by a lifetime of trips afield, a yellow Lab rests her weary bones.

A Man
and his Dog

by Ron Schara

R on Schara is a storyteller, a man fascinated with tales of the outdoors. For more than thirty years he has written about his days afield, often with a Lab by his side, for the Minneapolis *Star Tribune*. He also tells his tales to millions of television viewers through his shows *Minnesota Bound* on the Outdoor Life Network, *Call of the Wild* on the Outdoor Channel, and *Backroads with Ron & Raven* on ESPN. Raven is the current Lab in Ron's life, and Raven's name and likeness are nearly as well known as the author himself.

But before Raven, Ron shared his life with another Lab, Kyla. For many years, Kyla was Ron's companion afield (and just about everywhere else) as he pursued game throughout the Midwest. This is the story of Kyla, a dedicated hunter to the end.

A well-camouflaged hunter and his Lab take to the water in pursuit of ducks.

As the days cool and the leaves begin to fall, there is something in the air that is not seen.

Most of us who hunt know when it happens, although the source remains a mystery. Maybe it's the twinge in the air. Or the changing autumn landscape. Or the fall shuffle of wild game along with an inner clock of my own species that sparks something.

As a hunter, I only feel it.

Kyla, the black Lab, could smell it.

But for both of us the message was the same: It was time to go hunting.

Nothing else explains Kyla's sudden left turn out of the kennel the other day. After days, weeks and months of turning right and running to her usual "go potty" spot, Kyla charged to her left for a quick sniff at the back door of the Jeep.

She bounded back and yipped once.

I didn't have to tell her I'd loaded the Jeep with a portable crate and a shotgun. Her nose told her.

It was opening day of Minnesota's pheasant season.

It was also our eleventh October as hunting companions. As we roamed the tall CRP grass, I followed Kyla, watching her twitching tail, as usual. Her tail always said what she couldn't. It told of birds close or long gone. And at times, despite hours of fruitless hunting, her tail told of not quitting.

Kyla wore her heart on her tail. Most hunting dogs do.

In fact, it's this sense of teamwork that makes the hunter-dog bond so strong. In this fraternity, there are good hunting dogs and some not so good. We've hunted with both.

But every hunting dog is worth braggin' and boastin' about. Why? Because the team—hunter and dog—has slogged through the same marsh muck, shivered in the same cold and thirsted in the heat.

Together, hunter and dog have watched the same sunrises and shared the same sandwiches. And their hearts have been fluttered by the same gaudy ringnecks.

As a teammate, Kyla was always good company. She was, in fact, the best hunting dog that ever heeled at my side. She was all a retriever should be, with a good nose and a willingness to fetch forever. Kyla also did what most retrievers don't do: She pointed—stiff as a statue—if the bird held tight.

She also was an agreeable teammate. She knew when to be quiet in the car during long drives to pheasant country. She knew it didn't pay to whine with anticipation until the roads turned to gravel, or worse.

Kyla wasn't perfect, of course. She never came into season so she never had puppies. She knew a blast of the whistle meant "sit," but she sometimes didn't hear it. Dog trainer Tom Dokken used to say, "Kyla is a high-maintenance dog." It was a kind way of saying Kyla often forgot who was supposed to be in charge.

No, she wasn't perfect, but awfully close to it, if you don't mind a little bragging.

Retrieving a pheasant to hand.

Last week, Kyla and I headed for South Dakota for a jaunt in what can be the utopia of bird land. On the first afternoon, west of Redfield, Kyla rousted three ringnecks and I took three shots for our three-bird limit. What a team.

It should be noted, we also were hunting slower and easier. Neither of us was as young as we used to be. At the age of 10½, Kyla's muzzle had turned gray and her pace was of an elderly canine.

In the glow of our successful first-day hunt together, I silently wondered if this might be Kyla's last year as a member of the team. Even the thought of it was painful.

Last year or not, we would hunt again tomorrow.

It was late in the afternoon, hot and dry, when we joined up with friends for a walk into a vast field of CRP land near Pierre, South Dakota. Within the first 200 yards, a flock of pheasants burst into the air. Somebody dropped a ringneck, and Kyla fetched the dead bird to me.

She was panting hard from the heat. Twenty-five minutes later, Kyla's panting had turned to heavy heaving of her lungs. She refused water. Suddenly, she quit walking. We rushed Kyla to be cooled off in a farm pond. Gradually, her panting slowed, but her back legs were paralyzed. Heat stroke? Heart attack?

"It could have been both; the symptoms are classic," said Kyla's vet, Norb Epping of Coon Rapids, Minnesota.

Several hours later, Kyla seemed to be recovering. She was laying upright, her eyes watching my every move.

"You gonna be OK?" I asked.

For the answer I looked at Kyla's tail, the tail that told all. It didn't move.

Early the next morning, Kyla died.

"Kyla went the way she would have wanted to go, hunting," Epping said.

Yes, but the rest of the team is hurting.

ABOVE: *A little sleepy, but still inherently sleek, a black Lab waits patiently along a northern Minnesota stream.*
OVERLEAF: *A father and son head home after a day's hunting with their black Lab.*

ABOUT THE EDITOR AND PHOTOGRAPHERS

Todd R. Berger is the editor of the anthologies *Love of Labs, Love of Goldens, Love of Dogs, Love of German Shepherds, Love of Spaniels, Majestic Elk, Majestic Mule Deer,* and *100 Years of Hunting.* He is the acquisitions editor for Voyageur Press and a Minnesota-based freelance writer. *(Photograph © Tim Berger)*

Alan and Sandy Carey are freelance photographers based in Montana. Their images have been published in *National Geographic, Life, Audubon, Natural History, Readers Digest, Newsweek, Smithsonian, Ranger Rick, Time,* and numerous other magazines. They were the sole photographers for the Voyageur Press bestseller *Love of Goldens,* and their images have appeared in dozens of other books, as well as in calendars and greeting card collections. *(Photograph © Christina Carey)*